RETIREMENT
CALCULATOR

HOW MUCH MONEY DO I NEED TO RETIRE?

JASON R. PARKER

Retirement Calculator
How much money do I need to retire?
Copyright © 2022 by Jason R. Parker.

Address all inquiries to:
Jason R. Parker
9230 Bayshore Drive NW, Silverdale, WA 98383
360-337-2701 | info@parker-financial.net
www.retirementbudgetcalculator.com
www.parker-financial.net
www.soundretirementplanning.com

ISBN: 9798841614555
Imprint: Independently published

Published by: Jason R. Parker

Contributing Author: Hannah Rounds
Editors: Heather Dawn Henrichsen, Kynsey Solaita, Sara McCluskey
Back Cover Photo: Nelsen's Photographic Design
Cover & Interior Book Design: Fusion Creative Works

Every attempt has been made to properly source all quotations.

Printed in the United States of America

First Edition

DISCLAIMER AND LIMIT OF LIABILITY

RETIREMENT BUDGET CALCULATOR

This book is a valuable resource, but is intended to serve as a complement to the online tools found at *RetirementBudgetCalculator.com*. This book aims to help you answer some of the most often asked questions and fill in the gaps that the calculator does not currently compute.

The Retirement Budget Calculator is designed for the do-it-yourself crowd and is a powerful online tool that can help you plan your retirement and help you know if you have enough money to last throughout your retirement years.

If you are a recent retiree or within 5 years of retirement, I highly recommend this book and the Retirement Budget Calculator to help you navigate your transition.

CONTENTS

Chapter 1

RETIREMENT

WHEN DO PEOPLE RETIRE?

According to a Gallup poll that was conducted in 2021, the average retirement age was 62. However, this does not mean that you have to retire at this age. You can retire earlier if you have enough money saved. You can also retire later if you want to continue working.

WHEN SHOULD YOU RETIRE?

The most important factor in deciding when to retire is whether or not you have saved enough money. There are several ways to calculate how much you will need for retirement, but a good rule of thumb is to have enough saved to replace 70-80% of your pre-retirement income. For example, if you had been earning $80,000 per year in your working years, then you would want to plan for $64,000 of income in retirement.

HOW TO FIGURE OUT IF YOU'VE SAVED ENOUGH?

The easiest formula for deciding if you have saved enough money is to calculate the gap between your guaranteed income and your retirement budget. For example, let's say you will have $30,000 per year of Social Security income and you have calculated your annual retirement budget to require $60,000. You would have a gap of $30,000. Next, you would multiply the gap number of $30,000 x 25 and this would tell you if you have saved enough. In this example, you would need $750,000 saved to have a comfortable retirement. This rule of 25 times your annual spending is based on the Trinity study[1] which attempts to determine safe withdrawal rates from investment portfolios.

AVOID THESE COMMON RETIREMENT MISTAKES?

Now that we know how to calculate how much money we need for retirement, let's look at some common mistakes people make when planning for their retirement.

One of the biggest mistakes is retiring too early, because in the Trinity study the assumption is that your money will need to last for a 30-year retirement. With people trying to retire early and with life expectancy rates rising, many of us can expect to live well into our 90s. This means that we need to make sure our retirement savings will last for 30-40 years or more.

Another mistake is not having a plan for inflation. Over time, the cost of living will go up and your retirement income needs to keep pace with inflation. One way to do this is by investing in things like real estate or stocks that have the potential to increase in value over time.

---

1   "Trinity study." Wikipedia, https://en.wikipedia.org/wiki/Trinity_study.

HOW DO YOU DETERMINE IF YOU CAN AFFORD TO RETIRE?

The most important factor in deciding whether or not you can afford to retire is how much money you spend. Track your spending for a month or two and see where your money goes. Once you have a good idea of your monthly expenses, you can start to figure out how much you will need in retirement. Today many banks and credit unions have apps that can help you track your spending. Quicken, Mint, and YNAB are tools that you can use to help you track where your money goes and once you have that nailed down you can input your expenses into Retirement Budget Calculator to finalize your budget.

WHAT SHOULD I DO ONE YEAR BEFORE RETIREMENT?

Now that you know how to calculate how much money you need for retirement and some of the common mistakes people make, let's look at what you should do one year before retirement.

One of the most important things you can do is to get your financial house in order. This means getting rid of any debt that you have and making sure you have a good budget that you stick to.

Be sure you have all your ducks in a row with your retirement savings. You need to know how much you've saved and where it's invested. You need to know if your asset allocation will fulfill your requirements. You should also be informed of the different types of retirement accounts available to you and know how they work. Learn the rules about when you can access those accounts and what the tax implications will be when you do. A great general resource is Investopedia.com.

Additionally, you will need to look into your will and estate planning documents. This includes things like your power of attorney, healthcare directive, and beneficiary designations. It is also important to think about how you will want to spend your time in retirement. Many people find that they have more time on their hands once they retire, which can be good or bad depending on how you look at it. Try to have some hobbies and activities lined up that you can do in retirement. This will help you to stay active and avoid getting bored and spending money.

HOW MUCH HAVE YOU SAVED?

Do you have a 401k? Do you know how much is in it and what the rules are for withdrawing money from it? Do you have an IRA? What about a Roth IRA or an HSA?

Consider all of your retirement savings accounts that you could access if you were required to do so. Consider not just your retirement accounts, but also all of the money in your bank and brokerage accounts.

The most frequent mistake is to include the value of your house in the calculation. While your house is certainly an asset to include in your net worth, it is not generally thought of as a liquid investment as you would need to either sell the house or take out a loan to access the equity to help with your retirement living expenses.

HOW LONG DOES YOUR MONEY NEED TO LAST?

This is a question that you need to answer for yourself. It depends on a number of factors including how long you expect to live, how much money you will need to cover your expenses, and what kind of lifestyle you want in retirement.

Some people plan to retire later and may only need their savings to last for 20-30 years. Other people plan to retire sooner and may need their retirement savings to last for 30-40 years or longer.

The life expectancy calculator[2] that was developed by Social Security is a decent place to start.

IS IT BETTER TO TAKE SOCIAL SECURITY AT 62, 67, OR 70?

This is a question that many people ask and there is no easy answer. The best answer for you will depend on several factors including your age, health, marital status, and how much money you have saved for retirement.

If you start taking Social Security at 62 rather than waiting until you are at the full retirement age, then you will receive a reduced monthly benefit. If you plan to live a long time and have a family history of longevity, then you might wish to postpone beginning Social Security until age 70 and accrue delayed retirement credits. Your full retirement age is determined by the year you were born. If you were born between 1943-1954 your full retirement age is 66. The full retirement age increases gradually for those born

---

2   "Retirement & Survivors Benefits: Life Expectancy Calculator." Social Security, https://www.ssa.gov/oact/population/longevity.html.

between 1955-1960. Anyone born after 1960 has a full retirement age that is payable at 67. If your full retirement age is 67, but you wait until age 70 to start receiving your benefit, then you will accrue an 8% increase in your retirement benefits per year.

SOCIAL SECURITY TAXES

One of the reasons to optimize your Social Security retirement benefits is it enjoys special rules regarding federal income taxes. The provisional income rules say that none of your Social Security payments may be taxed to a maximum of 85% of your benefits. The taxation of Social Security benefits will in part be determined by other sources of taxable income. For example, dividends and interest income count, but qualified Roth IRA withdrawals do not count when figuring out how much of your Social Security is taxable. In the Retirement Budget Calculator, we automatically do the provisional income calculations to determine how much of your Social Security will be taxable. The calculator also allows you to modify the withdrawal order so that you can see how taking income from a traditional IRA compares with a Roth IRA to impact the taxation of your Social Security. If you have not yet signed up for the Retirement Budget Calculator you can use this free calculator to help you with the provisional income tax calculations.

The Social Security benefit was developed by actuaries. If you start benefits early, you will take a reduced benefit, but receive more payments. Whereas, if you wait to start Social Security benefits until age 70, you get a higher benefit but Social Security will make payments for a shorter period. The Social Security Administration developed its formula to pay an equal amount of income over average life expectancy, regardless of when you start benefits. Because single individuals must live past age 80 for it to make sense to delay Social Security, and because married couples' break-even analysis is more difficult due to survivor benefits available, you'll want to build a customized Social Security plan for your unique scenario, whether you're married or single. The Social Security Administration does not have any personal information about your particular life expectancy, so having a thorough grasp of your family's history may assist you in calculating when to claim your Social Security benefits.

The decision of when to start Social Security is a personal one and you should consider all of the factors mentioned above before making a decision. There is no right or wrong answer, but there is an answer that is best for you.

PLAN FOR THE GO-GO, SLOW-GO, AND NO-GO YEARS

It is important to plan for all three phases of retirement – the go-go years, the slow-go years, and the no-go years.

- **The go-go years** are typically the years when you first retire and you have good health, a spouse, friends, and travel is fun. This is the time do as much as you can and are the best years to travel and explore.

- **The slow-go years** are the years where you may start to experience health issues or the loss of a spouse and travel may not be as fun.

- **The no-go years** are usually the consequence of poor health, a lack of resources, a lack of desire, or both. These years could involve a time when medical expenses are higher and you may not be able to travel as much.

No matter what phase of retirement you are in, it is important to have a plan and to think about how your spending will change in each phase. Each phase presents different challenges and opportunities. By planning for all three phases, you can make the most of your retirement years.

Chapter 2

ACHIEVING FINANCIAL INDEPENDENCE

Financial independence is one of the most enticing phrases in the personal finance lexicon. For some people, financial independence means escaping a paycheck-to-paycheck cycle. Others think of it as being fabulously wealthy and owning yachts on the Riviera. While each definition is valid in its own way, this chapter focuses on financial independence for retirement.

As it relates to retirement, financial independence is having enough money or passive cash flow to cover all reasonable expenses for the rest of your life. Retirees who achieve financial independence before retiring don't need to worry about returning to work.

If you're approaching a traditional (or early) retirement age, it's worth checking whether you're also approaching your financial independence number (FI number). Or more accurately, your FI numbers, plural. We cover the six most important numbers to track to ensure you hit financial independence before retiring.

THE FI NUMBER

The basic FI number shows whether you have enough saved to retire. To calculate it, you need to know your annual expenses (which can be found through the Retirement Budget Calculator).

Once you know your annual expenses, you need to compare them to your assets.

When your guaranteed annual income sources (Social Security, pension, rental income, etc.) and 3.5% of your investment portfolio are greater than your annual expenses, you are financially independent.

The 3.5% of assets is considered a conservative or "safe" withdrawal rate for someone who expects to need to live off their assets for at least 30 years.

Let's say a couple has expenses of $90,000 per year. When they turn 62, they expect to have the following guaranteed income sources in retirement:

- Wife Social Security: $2,000 per month or $24,000 per year

- Husband Social Security: $1,300 per month or $15,600 per year

- Husband pension: $500 per month or $6,000 per year

- Rental property net income: $2,000 per month or $24,000 per year

In total, they have $67,600 in Guaranteed Income. On top of this, the couple has $400,000 in retirement savings accounts, 3.5% of $400,000 is $14,000 per year.

Their FI Number is: $67,600 in income + $14,000 in safe withdrawals = $81,600 in total income. Total spending ($90,000) - expected retirement income ($81,6000) = negative $8,400.

According to this formula, the couple has a gap of $8,400 per year to cover before hitting FI. To formally hit FI before retirement, the couple can lower expenses or increase their savings. Playing with the numbers in the Retirement Budget Calculator can help them decide which makes more sense for them.

"SAFE" WITHDRAWAL RATIO

During retirement, a portion of the retiree's spending will be covered by guaranteed income and the other part covered by withdrawing from a portfolio. During the first several years of retirement, financial planners typically advise retirees to have withdrawal rates ranging from 3-4% of their portfolio annually. This is considered a "safe" withdrawal rate. When they withdraw at this rate, retirees are unlikely to run out of money during a 30-year retirement assuming a 60/40 stock bond asset allocation (60% invested in stocks, 40% invested in bonds).

The Retirement Budget Calculator helps users calculate their withdrawal ratio. Ideally, users will want to keep their ratio below 4% for most of their retirement. This ratio is especially important during the early years of retirement, when retirees have longer to live and therefore need their portfolio to last longer.

RETIREMENT SAVINGS RATIO

Closely related to the FI number is the "retirement savings ratio". This number tells you how much more you need to save to reach financial independence before retirement.

The retirement savings number can be calculated as follows:

Annual essential expenses – annual guaranteed income = annual portfolio withdrawals.

Portfolio withdrawals are the amount you will withdraw from your portfolio each year. Multiplying the annual withdrawals by 25 to 33 gives you the nest egg you need to retire.

The couple in the example above has $67,600 in "guaranteed income" per year of retirement but they spend $90,000 per year.

The couple needs to withdraw $22,400 per year ($90,000-$67,600) with their current spending plan. For a 4% annual withdrawal rate, they need a portfolio with $560,000 ($22,400 X 25). If they want a more conservative 3% withdrawal rate, they need $745,920 ($22,400 X 33.3).

MILLIONAIRE NEXT DOOR FORMULA

A related formula is the Millionaire Next Door Formula.[3] This formula doesn't track retirement readiness or financial independence. Instead, it shows your likelihood of becoming a "Millionaire Next Door".

---

3   Stanley, Thomas J., and William D. Danko. The Millionaire Next Door: The Surprising Secrets of America's Wealthy. Taylor Trade Publishing, 2010

This formula suggests that you should multiply your current annual income by your age and divide that by 10. The number remaining is a good target for your nest egg.

A couple whose average age is 58 has a household income of $150,000. 58 X $150,000 = $8,700,000. Divided by 10 leaves them with a target net worth of $870,000.

Ideally, this couple will have a nest egg with at least $870,000 in it by age 58. If you're "behind" according to this goal, don't despair! Many people face lower incomes and higher expenses during their 30s and 40s when they have children in the home. Others experience unsuccessful businesses for several years before they start a better earning trajectory. Your 50s and 60s are an excellent opportunity to strengthen earning potential and boost investment rates.

SECURE INCOME SCORE

While the FI number provides a technical angle to retirement readiness, it's not the only angle to consider. Retirees will also want to consider how comfortable they feel spending money during retirement. Many people are more comfortable spending income (from Social Security, pensions, and possibly rental properties) than selling assets to cover their regular expenses during retirement.

The Secure Income Score takes this into account. The Secure Income Score divides your income from guaranteed sources by your essential expenses during retirement. The Retirement Budget Calculator actually looks over the decades of your intended retirement to come up with this calculation.

Ideally, retirees will want at least 80% of their essential (non-negotiable) expenses to be covered by guaranteed income. If your Secure Income Score is well below the 80% threshold, then you may have options to boost it before retirement. For example, paying off your mortgage and all other debts before retirement can lower essential expenses. Retirees with large nest eggs may want to convert a portion of their nest egg to a guaranteed annuity to boost their income.

DEBT TO ASSETS RATIO

During the final five to ten years before retirement, it is important to take a look at your total debt picture. Most people want to retire debt-free. Having lots of payments can make it difficult to squeeze in some of the luxuries that will make retirement fun.

While paying off debt before retirement is important, it may be just as important to avoid taking on excessive debt before or during retirement. Big-ticket purchases like a new RV or helping children pay for school may be important to you, but these purchases can be tough on the retirement budget.

If you're planning to retire soon, work to keep your debt-to-assets ratio below 20%. Your debt is your total debt load. Your assets are all your assets that are invested in either cash or other financial securities like the stock market.

People with higher debt loads may want to downsize or consider working longer to lower their debt.

ARE YOU PREPARING FOR FINANCIAL INDEPENDENCE?

Financial independence before retirement is a worthy goal. Achieving financial independence before retirement can help you get the most out of your retirement years. It will allow you to spend less time worrying about finances and more time living a meaningful life. Start tracking your FI numbers today so you can retire with confidence down the road.

Chapter 3

NET WORTH - HOW DO YOU COMPARE?

Since 1989, the Federal Reserve has conducted a Survey of Consumer Finances[4] and they update the survey every few years. As of the time I'm writing this, the most recent update to this survey was in 2019. As we look at the data, remember this quote: "Comparison is the thief of joy".

When we compare ourselves to others, it's easy to either feel good or bad about ourselves. The key is to focus on our journey and not worry about where others are.

So with that in mind, let's take a look at the median net worth for 2019.

- For those younger than age 35, the average net worth is $76,340

- For ages 35-44 the average net worth is $437,770

- For ages 45-54 the average net worth is $833,790

---

4 "The Fed - Table: Survey of Consumer Finances, 1989 - 2019." Board of Governors of the Federal Reserve System, https://www.federalreserve.gov/econres/scf/dataviz/ scf/table/#series:Net_Worth;demographic:agecl;population:all;units:mean;ran ge:1989,2019.

- For ages 55-64 the average net worth is $1,176,520

- For ages 65-74 the average net worth is $1,215,920

- For ages 75+ the average net worth is $958,450

WHY YOU NEED TO CALCULATE YOUR NET WORTH

Your net worth is the financial equivalent of looking in a mirror. When you look at your net worth, you start to see where you're doing well financially and where you're falling short. If you have the financial equivalent of a booger on your face, your net worth will show you that too.

Are you regularly calculating your net worth? Do you know how to calculate it? This chapter explains what net worth is, why it matters, and how to calculate it.

WHAT IS NET WORTH?

Your net worth is the value of your assets (what you own) less the value of liabilities (debts) that you owe. An easy formula for net worth is: Assets − Liabilities = Net Worth

The trick to calculating your net worth is understanding how to define assets and liabilities.

Simply put, assets are things you own that are worth money. Of course, assets include things like the value of your retirement accounts and your checking and savings accounts. But those aren't the only assets you need to consider. If you own property (such as a personal home or rental property), then you'll want to count those towards your net worth. Business owners should include a conservative estimate of the value of their business in their net worth. Assets can even include personal property such as vehicles, fine art, firearms collections, or rare coins.

Compared to your assets, liabilities tend to be more straightforward. These are any debts you owe including a mortgage, credit card debts, auto loans, or other debts.

WHY DOES NET WORTH MATTER FOR RETIREMENT PLANNING?

Retirement planning is an exercise in cash flow planning, but that doesn't mean your net worth is unimportant. During your working years, it's easy to focus on your income or your salary as the most important part of your financial life. However, if you plan to retire, you won't earn a salary (or a full-time income) any longer. You will use your assets to generate income, and your debts will be a drain on that income.

A growing net worth statement shows that you're on track to achieving your retirement lifestyle goals. Your net worth is a key indicator of your overall financial health, especially during your working years. That's why the Retirement Budget Calculator includes a net worth calculator for retirement.

HOW CAN YOU CALCULATE NET WORTH FOR RETIREMENT?

A net worth calculator for retirement makes it easy for you to calculate and track your net worth over time.

First, add up your assets. The Retirement Budget Calculator breaks your assets into four major categories which you can see below.

LIQUID INVESTABLE ASSETS

These are assets that are easy to convert to cash. They include the following types of accounts:

- Savings accounts

- Checking accounts

- Money Market Accounts

- Certificate of Deposits (CDs)

- Retirement accounts (IRAs, Roth IRAs, 401(k)s, etc.)

- Brokerage accounts with stocks and bonds

REAL ESTATE ASSETS

Real estate assets include any properties that you own which include the following assets:

- Your personal residence

- Rental properties

- Commercial property that you own

- Raw land

- Share in a privately held real estate investment trust (REIT)

PERSONAL PROPERTY

Personal property represents the value of things that you own. Technically, you could count the value of everything from your furniture to your old socks. However, most people just include the value of high-value personal items that they could easily sell. These include:

- Musical instruments

- Jewelry

- Furniture

- Hobby equipment (such as computers, stereos, tools, unused materials, etc.)

OTHER ASSETS

Other assets include those you own that aren't covered ("Trinity study") by other categories. Such as:

- Vehicles

- Recreational vehicles

- Collectibles

- Gold and Silver Bullion

- The estimated value of a business (that you can sell)

The value of all four categories represents your total assets.

NEXT, ADD UP YOUR LIABILITIES

Once you've established the value of your assets, you need to account for all your liabilities. These can include any of the following:

- Balance on any mortgages (including rental real estate)

- Home equity loans or lines of credit

- Credit card balances

- Auto loans

- Required alimony payments

- Required child support payments

- Judgments against you

Finally, subtract your liabilities from your assets

Once you know the value of your assets, and the value of your liabilities, calculating your net worth is easy. Simply use this formula: Assets - Liabilities = Net Worth

Retirement is all about cash flow, not net worth. If you have 10 million dollars in collectible baseball cards that don't make any money, it won't benefit your retirement cash flow unless you're willing to part with some of your collection.

Chapter 4

HOW LONG DOES YOUR MONEY NEED TO LAST?

If you're like the typical person, you probably have a good idea of when you want to retire. But have you put much thought into how long your retirement is set to last? Unlike a sabbatical or other major financial goals, it's not always clear how long it will last because your retirement timeline depends on your life expectancy. When you're thinking about retirement, it's important to consider your longevity.

ARE LIVES GETTING LONGER?

For decades, longer life spans seemed like a given. In the year 1900, a woman born in the United States of America (USA) could expect to reach an average age of 48.31. Fast forward sixty years, and a person born in the USA in 1960 had was expected to have an estimated average lifespan of 69.8 years according to data from the World Bank[5]. The trend of longevity marched upwards with rare

---

5 "Life expectancy at birth, total (years) | Data." World Bank Data, https://data. worldbank.org/indicator/SP.DYN.LE00.IN.

"Life expectancy at birth, at 65 years of age, and at 75 years of age, by race and sex." CDC, https://www.cdc.gov/nchs/data/hus/2010/022.pdf.

ticks downwards until the last five years. In 2014, life expectancy in the USA hit an all-time high (78.8 on average), and expectancy has plateaued or fallen in the subsequent years. While the plateau in life expectancy may be concerning, it is worth looking a bit deeper into the numbers. Between 2016 and 2017, death rates for 7 out of the 10 leading causes of death increased in the USA. The three causes that increased the most were flu and pneumonia (5.9%), unintentional injury such as a drug overdose (4.2%), and suicide (3.7%).[6]

Most health-related causes of death are difficult to avoid. But other causes, including unintentional injury and suicide, are somewhat more avoidable. These death causes are linked to the epidemics of drug use and loneliness. One key to living a longer and more fulfilling life is to plan for ways to stay engaged with your family and in building up your local community.

The steady march towards longer lives seems to have plateaued recently, but life expectancy is still near all-time highs. According to data from the Social Security Administration[7], 77% of men and 86% of women will live until their full retirement age of 67.

---

6   "Mortality in the United States, 2017." CDC, https://www.cdc.gov/nchs/data/databriefs/db328-h.pdf. .

7   "Actuarial Life Table." Social Security, https://www.ssa.gov/oact/STATS/table4c6.html.
    "Retirement & Survivors Benefits: Life Expectancy Calculator." Social Security, https://www.ssa.gov/OACT/population/longevity.html.

HOW MUCH LONGER DO YOU EXPECT TO LIVE?

Whether overall life expectancy is growing or plateaued is an important societal question. But for aspiring retirees, understanding their specific life expectancy is even more important than understanding the average life expectancy. When you're on the brink of retiring, it's helpful to understand if you're more likely to live to age 75 or age 105.

Nobody knows the answer for sure, but there are some methods for making a best guess. The Social Security Administration keeps lots of data on births, deaths, and longevity. You can use the life expectancy tool from them to estimate how much longer you'll live. According to the tool, a man born on January 21, 1959, can expect to live 22.2 more years from today, which puts his life expectancy at 83 years.

However, if he makes it to age 70, he will expect to live 15.8 more years to age 85.8.

Getting a good sense of your remaining life expectancy can help you make prudent planning decisions while also making the most of your life span. The Retirement Budget Calculator helps you plan cash flow throughout your retirement and it includes the ability to forecast your budget through the remainder of your lifespan.

It may seem odd to predict the date of your death, but knowing your life expectancy can help you predict whether you'll outlive your savings or your savings will outlive you.

WILL YOU OUTLIVE YOUR SAVINGS?

While data from the Social Security Administration isn't a perfect way to estimate the length of your retirement, it is a useful place to start. When you use the Retirement Budget Calculator, you can see a table that forecasts your cash inflows and outflows throughout the remainder of your expected life.

If the Retirement Budget Calculator shows that your nest egg dips below $0 before your expected death (or your partner's expected death), then you run a high risk of running out of money during retirement.

In 1969, when life expectancy was just 69 years, saving for 4-5 years of additional life may have been sufficient for retirement. But today, most people who live to retirement age will make it to age 85 or older. Adjusting your cash inflows (by working longer or saving more now) or your outflows (by cutting back on discretionary expenses) can help you find a way for your money to last the two decades or more that it may need to last.

ARE YOUR RETIREMENT SAVINGS LIKELY TO OUTLIVE YOU?

Less frequently, you may be someone who realizes that your retirement savings are very likely to outlive you. Perhaps the Social Security Administration estimates you have 17 more years to live, but the Retirement Budget Calculator shows that you have enough money to last until age 120. What should you do?

Seeing the excess cash flow may convince you that spending extra money today to enjoy time with loved ones or to indulge in a passion (such as travel or expensive vehicles) could be well worth the money.

PLANNING FOR YOUR REAL LIFE EXPECTANCY IN RETIREMENT

No retirement plan can be perfect, but avoiding the reality of your longevity will not help you one bit. The Retirement Budget Calculator can help you take a detailed look at your spending habits, your expected income in retirement, and your expected lifespan. It can give you a more detailed view of how your finances are likely to look in retirement.

Whether you're already retired, planning to retire soon, or still a few decades away from retirement, understanding your expected longevity can help you plan for a rich life today and for years to come during retirement.

Chapter 5

RETIREMENT SPENDING

When planning for retirement, it is important to include all of your potential expenses. This can be tricky, as there are many different factors to consider. In this chapter, we will discuss the 7 categories of retirement expenses and then provide a list of 65 specific expenses you will want to include in your retirement spending plan. By taking into account all of these costs, you can create a realistic plan that will help you enjoy a comfortable retirement!

7 CATEGORIES OF RETIREMENT EXPENSES

- Housing

- Loans and Liabilities

- Food and Personal Care

- Insurance and Medical

- Vehicles and Transportation

- Travel and Entertainment

- Giving and Miscellaneous

Now let's look at the retirement expenses you'll want to include in each category.

Housing

Here is the data provided in the Retirement Budget Calculator's template. You may add and delete data to make your retirement expenditure strategy unique to you.

- Real Estate Taxes
- HOA Dues
- Electric
- Garbage
- Water
- Sewer
- Natural Gas
- Cable
- Internet
- Cell Phone
- Home Phone
- Security System
- Home Improvements
- Furniture
- Yard Maintenance

Loans and Liabilities

- House Mortgage

- Auto Loan

- Boat Loan

- Credit Card

- RV / Camping Trailer

- Student Loan

- Alimony

- Child Support

Food and Personal Care

- Groceries

- Restaurants

- Spending Cash

- Haircuts and Nails

- Dry Cleaning

- Pet Food and Medicine

- Gym Membership

- Clothes and Shoes

- Chiropractor

Insurance and Medical

- Auto Insurance

- HomeOwners Insurance

- Health Insurance

- Dental Insurance

- Life Insurance

- Long Term Care Insurance

- Medicare Supplemental Insurance

- Vision and Eyecare

- Medications

Vehicles and Transportation

- Annual Tuneup

- Fuel

- Oil Change

- Maintenance

- Tires

- Repairs

- Memberships

- License Renewal

- Public Transportation

Travel and Entertainment

- Vacations

- Birthdays

- Christmas

- Anniversary

- Amazon Prime

- Hobbies and Lessons

- Magazines and Newspapers

- Software Subscriptions

- Netflix

- Movie Rentals

Giving and Miscellaneous

- Tithes and Offerings

- Missions

- Charitable Donations

- Financial Advisor

- Tax Preparation

REMEMBER TO INCLUDE TAXES

We all know taxes are a necessary evil, but did you know that they can also be a significant expense in retirement? That's right, taxes can eat up a good chunk of your retirement income if you're not careful. You will want to include both state and federal taxes in your retirement spending planning.

There are a few ways to reduce the amount of taxes you'll owe in retirement. One is to consider doing Roth IRA contributions and conversions as you prepare for retirement. Another is to carefully plan your withdrawals from those accounts so that you don't end up in a higher than necessary tax bracket.

ESSENTIAL VS DISCRETIONARY EXPENSES

The Retirement Budget Calculator can help you figure out how much you need to spend in retirement and you can tag your expenses as either essential or discretionary. Here's a quick rundown of the difference between essential and discretionary expenses:

Essential expenses are those that you need to live, such as food, shelter, and clothing.

Discretionary expenses are those that you can live without, such as entertainment and vacations.

Some people choose to retire on a shoestring budget by eliminating all nonessential expenditures. Because you didn't work hard to get to retirement only to survive, most individuals will want to include discretionary expenses.

THE GOAL OF RETIREMENT

The goal of retirement is cash flow. It's all about making sure you have enough income to cover your expenses. You can start to project how much income you'll have in retirement and then compare your guaranteed income to your costs. Some of the most common sources of income in retirement are Social Security benefits, pensions, annuities, or rental income.

THE GAP

Normally, your income sources will not cover all of your expenses in retirement. This is where your retirement savings come into play. You will likely need to supplement your income with withdrawals from a 401k, IRA, or other retirement accounts.

After entering all of your income and expenses into the Retirement Budget Calculator, let's say you discover that you will have $50,000 of income every year but your expenses are $90,000 per year. The gap in this scenario is $40,000, which is the difference between how much income you have compared to how much you plan to spend.

HAVE YOU SAVED ENOUGH TO COVER THE GAP?

The general rule of thumb is that you will take the gap number and multiply it by 25. This is based on the 4% rule that says you can safely withdraw up to 4% of your retirement savings each year without depleting your account. In the example above, you would need one million dollars saved to cover the $40,000 gap.

Chapter 6

SOCIAL SECURITY

THE TOP FOUR QUESTIONS TO ASK BEFORE TAKING SOCIAL SECURITY

Nearly 90% of all Americans age 65 and older receive Social Security income. For most retirees, this income plays a significant role in their retirement budget. But deciding when to take Social Security benefits can be a challenge. The nuts and bolts of the program are difficult to understand, and each person's retirement plan is unique. Despite the many moving pieces, the Retirement Budget Calculator can give users insights that can help them gain confidence about when and how to start taking Social Security. There are four important factors to consider when building Social Security income into your retirement budget.[8]

---

8   Parker, Jason R. "The top four questions to ask before taking Social Security." Retirement Budget Calculator, 20 January 2021, https://retirementbudgetcalculator. com/blog.php?post=no-retirement-budget-is-complete-without-factoring.

1. Can I Cover The Gap?

According to the Social Security Administration, Social Security income accounts for a third of all income among the elderly. One out of two married couples and 70% of unmarried individuals rely on Social Security for the majority of their income. If you're not working, there's a good chance that you'll need Social Security income to cover the gaps in your budget. The Retirement Budget Calculator can help you with the cash flow planning aspect of this exercise. It can show you a year-by-year or even month-by-month short-fall in your cash flow.

Those who can't draw down from savings to cover the gap will likely need to tighten the belt or start taking Social Security as soon as their paychecks stop coming. Retirees can begin taking Social Security at age 62, but that is considered early retirement. If you start taking the checks at age 62, your retirement benefit will be reduced by 25-30% depending on your full retirement age. To receive your full benefits, you have to wait until the full retirement age which isn't until 66 or 67 (for those born after 1960). For example, a person who expected to receive $2,000 in benefits at their full retirement age of 67 would receive just $1,400 per month if they started taking benefits at age 62.

Even people who plan to take benefits starting at age 62 may need to prepare to cover an income gap if they stop working the month they turn 62.

Social Security is paid one month behind. The January 2021 benefits are paid in February 2021. A person who wants to start receiving benefits in January won't see their first check until February. The exact date of the first check depends on your birth date within the month. People with birthdays between the 1st and 10th of the month are paid on the Second Wednesday of the month. Those with birthdays between the 11th and 20th receive checks on the 3rd Wednesday of the month. Those with later birthdays receive their checks on the 4th Wednesday of the month.

2. How Long Can I Expect To Live?

People who have the means to cover living expenses until their full retirement age (or beyond) can be a bit more strategic about when they take benefits. One calculation that many financial planners recommend is a "break-even analysis".

If you begin taking benefits at age 62, you'll receive extra money from age 62 through 67. But from age 67 to the end of your life, you'll receive fewer benefits.

Of course, nobody knows the number of their days. But the Retirement Budget Calculator uses longevity information from the Social Security Administration to suggest the average length of life you can expect to live, given your current age. The average 65-year-old can expect to live a full two decades more. That means, over the lifespan of a typical person, taking benefits at full retirement age yields more benefits than taking benefits earlier.

If you're conducting a "formal" break-even analysis using the Retirement Budget Calculator, remember to factor in the option for Delayed Retirement Credits[9]. Each month that you delay taking Social Security (after your full retirement age), you can receive a 0.67% increase in your benefits (8% per year). This 8% growth is allowed until age 70. Those with a full retirement age of 67 can receive up to 24% more income per check by waiting until age 70.

3. How Much Life-Quality Can I Get From My Social Security Income?

Of course, life isn't only about money. Some retirees, especially those with high income or high net worth, may choose to take Social Security early because it can provide "fun money" earlier in retirement. During the first decade of retirement, you may have more physical health to engage in various activities. Perhaps you want to travel, rent an RV, play pickleball, golf at a fancy club, or go sky-diving. Taking Social Security income earlier can give you disposable income to enjoy while you still have peak health.

4. Will The Social Security Program Even Be Around By My Full Retirement Age?

According to the Social Security Administration, the Social Security Trust Fund is expected to be depleted by the year 2035. At that point, benefits will be reduced by 21%. At this time, the Social Security Program as a whole seems politically stable. It is unlikely for the whole program to disappear in 2035.

---

9 "Benefits Planner: Retirement | Delayed Retirement Credits | SSA." Social Security, https://www.ssa.gov/benefits/retirement/planner/delayret.html.

But if benefits will be cut in 2035, should you take your benefits early? Taking benefits early (at age 62) reduces benefits by 25-30%. If benefits are reduced in 2035, the effect of the cut is compounded by an already lower payment. This could work for a few people who don't expect to live particularly long lives. However, a formal break-even analysis may be required to decide what makes sense for you.

To do the break-even analysis in the Retirement Budget Calculator, run the numbers both ways. First, see your income and net worth if you begin withdrawing at age 62. Remember to cut your benefits by 21% starting in 2035.

Then run the numbers as if you begin receiving income at your full retirement age. Again cut benefits by 21% starting in 2035. For those with expected lifespans that extend well beyond 2035, delaying Social Security is likely to make more sense. However, some people may find that withdrawing at 62 makes more sense.

RUN THE NUMBERS, BUT DON'T LET THE NUMBERS RUN YOU

At the end of the day, only you can decide when to take Social Security. The Retirement Budget Calculator can help inform your retirement planning. It can help you iron out critical cash flow details. But your retirement budget is just one part of your retirement planning. Make sure you're taking all parts of your life into account as you step towards the next phase of life.

Chapter 7

RETIREMENT WITHDRAWAL STRATEGIES

During retirement, most people want to spend their time with the people they love, and spend their money in a way that brings meaning to them. Most want to enjoy a lifestyle similar to their pre-retirement standard of living, but they don't want to be a retail greeter at age 85 because they've run out of money. Figuring out strategies to manage cash flow throughout a decades-long retirement is no easy task. Each retiree will need to take an individualized approach to manage their retirement funds for the long haul. However, many well-researched retirement withdrawal strategies aim to help retirees manage their money during retirement. If you're starting to think about retirement, considering a withdrawal strategy could make sense for you.

BEFORE THINKING ABOUT WITHDRAWAL STRATEGIES

The withdrawal strategies laid out below differ, but most share a common foundation. To successfully implement strategies, retirees and their financial advisors need a solid understanding of their personal finances. These are a few key numbers that people need to know before figuring out retirement withdrawal strategies.

Annual spending.

This figure represents the total you plan to spend in a typical year. The Retirement Budget Calculator allows users to forecast their spending (including expected inflation) throughout their lifetime.

Discretionary vs. Necessary spending.

During retirement, certain expenses such as food and medical care are necessary for retirees. However, other expenses are discretionary. Marking clear boundaries between necessary and discretionary expenses makes it easier for retirees to consider what costs they may be willing to cut during an under-performing market.

Total spendable assets.

This is the amount of money in retirement, brokerage, and other cash accounts. If you plan to sell a major asset (such as real estate) before retirement, you may want to include the value of that asset here.

Expected guaranteed income during retirement.

Most people will have some sort of guaranteed income during retirement. This includes income from government pensions (Social Security), workplace pensions, annuities, and any other form of income that you expect to last during retirement.

The Retirement Budget Calculator can help you get to all of these numbers on a personal level. Having that information at the ready can make it easier to put your numbers into some of the examples.

THE 4% RULE

One of the best-known retirement withdrawal strategies is called the 4% rule (as previously mentioned earlier). Under this withdrawal strategy, retirees withdraw 4% of their portfolio the first year of retirement. In subsequent years, they increase the amount they withdraw by inflation (Consumer Price Index for All Urban Consumers or CPI-U).

For example, a couple that has $1 million invested would withdraw $40,000 in their first year of retirement. If inflation is 3%, the next year they will withdraw $41,200. Over time, their withdrawals only change based on inflation. The performance of the market does not play into their withdrawal strategies.

Some people call this rule the "4% safe withdrawal rate". This indicates that retirees using this strategy have a low likelihood of running out of money during a 30-year retirement. While no withdrawal strategy is perfectly safe, this one tends to be more conservative than some of the other strategies.

This strategy was initially developed by William Bengen[10] in the late 1990s. He based his initial work on a 30-year time horizon. Later on, Bengen expanded his study to include more asset classes and different investment mixes. In the later studies, Bengen concluded that withdrawal rates may be somewhat higher than the 4% rule. However, the rule itself is still called the 4% rule.

---

10 Bengen, William P. "DETERMINING WITHDRAWAL RATES USING HISTORICAL DATA." Retail Investor .org, https://www.retailinvestor.org/pdf/ Bengen1.pdf.

People who are planning their own withdrawal strategy may be attracted to this strategy because of its simplicity. Retirees only need to watch inflation to figure out the amount to withdraw. However, this strategy may be best suited to high-net-worth retirees who can manage their expenditures on a relatively low percentage of their portfolio.

BUCKETS STRATEGY

The buckets strategy is a retirement withdrawal strategy that helps retirees segment their money based on time. Under this strategy, funds needed in the short term are invested very conservatively. It may be in CDs, Treasury bonds, or other investments expected to have low volatility. Long-term money can be invested more aggressively, even in stocks.

The amount of money in each bucket depends on the retiree's expected spending over different time horizons. For example, a retiree who needs to withdraw $20,000 per year may have between $60,000 and $100,000 in a short-term account. The remainder may be invested in moderate or more aggressive investments.

Because money needed in the short-term is conservatively invested, retirees may feel more comfortable with volatility in their long-term investment bucket. By allowing some money to remain in growth-oriented investments, retirees are more likely to see their overall returns exceed inflation in the long term. The Retirement Budget Calculator offers a "Buckets" visualization for users. This may help guide users to think about matching their time and financial risk profiles. This bucket investment strategy is generally the most helpful for retirees who have variable needs over time, and want their withdrawal strategy to reflect those needs.

We'll discuss the buckets strategy in more detail in Chapter 8.

GUYTON-KLINGER DYNAMIC SPENDING

Dynamic spending withdrawal strategies aren't quite as simple as the strategies outlined above. Under dynamic spending strategies, retirees may have the freedom to spend a bit more liberally during their first year of retirement. However, they must adjust spending based on market conditions and inflation. High inflation combined with a down market may lead to some belt-tightening during the retirement years.

The Guyton-Klinger Dynamic Spending strategy[11] starts out fairly simply. Retirees may withdraw between 5.8% and 6.2% of their portfolio in the first year of retirement. The actual amount of withdrawal depends on the retiree's strategy. If the market goes up, then the retiree adjusts their withdrawal for inflation. However, if the market drops, the withdrawal amount freezes.

For example, a person with a $1 million portfolio may withdraw $62,000 in the first year of retirement. The next year, if the market

---

11 Guyton, Jonathan T., and William J. Klinger. "CFP." Cornerstone Wealth Advisors, https://cornerstonewealthadvisors.com/wp-content/uploads/2014/09/08-06_ WebsiteArticle.pdf. – see methodology on pag 51.

is up, and inflation was 3%, the retiree withdraws $63,860. If the market subsequently falls, the withdrawal freezes at $63,860. The withdrawal amount remains frozen until the market has a positive annual return. After that, the retiree can adjust the $63,860 by the amount of inflation that year.

This dynamic withdrawal strategy also has exacting strategies for how retirees should rebalance each year, and which asset class should support their withdrawal.

The Guyton-Klinger Dynamic Spending withdrawal strategy looks over 40-year retirement windows. Jonathan Guyton and William Klinger set their rules based on a 1973-1974 retirement date. Based on a double whammy of poor market performance and inflation, this was statistically the "worst time to retire" in recent times. They then tested the rules using a more robust statistical method.

While the dynamic spending strategy rules are complex, they may be appealing to retirees who hope to spend more during the early retirement years. We are not aware of a dynamic withdrawal strategy calculator so retirees may consider consulting a fiduciary financial planner to help them execute this withdrawal strategy. In some cases, the actual implementation of the strategy may look a lot like the "buckets" approach to withdrawals. That includes more conservative investments for shorter-term investing and more aggressive investments for money needed in more than a decade.

VANGUARD DYNAMIC SPENDING

The Vanguard Dynamic Spending[12] withdrawal strategy seeks a middle ground between portfolio longevity and spending freedom. This approach recognizes that retirees would like to spend more money if it is available due to market conditions, but they may be willing to cut back if market conditions require it.

Under this paradigm, retirees withdraw a set percentage of their portfolio each year (say 5%). However, the percentage a retiree withdraws never increases by more than 5% from the previous year. Likewise, it never falls below -1.5% of spending from the previous year. If the portfolio grows by 10% in the second year of retirement, the retiree will increase withdrawals by 5%. If it decreases by -10% the following year, she will decrease withdrawals by -1.5%.

This strategy assumes that retirees have some flexibility in their spending. If every dollar in a retiree's budget goes towards necessities, a -1.5% decrease in withdrawals could be a problem for that retiree (especially if it is paired with inflation).

REQUIRED MINIMUM DISTRIBUTIONS (RMD) RULE

The Required Minimum Distributions (RMD) approach to withdrawal bases withdrawals on the retiree's life expectancy and

---

12 "A rule for all seasons: Vanguard's dynamic approach to retirement spending." Vanguard Canada, https://www.vanguard.ca/documents/literature/dynamic-ret-spending-paper.pdf.

the present value of the portfolio. Under this strategy, retirees withdraw based on a Uniform Lifetime Table[13]. The Uniform Lifetime Table adds ten years to retirees' expected lifespan, which is considered the distribution period. The value of the portfolio is divided by the distribution period to determine the annual withdrawals.

Early in retirement, the withdrawals will be a low percentage of the portfolio value (even less than 4% early on). While later in retirement, the percentage of withdrawals increases (if you make it to 115, you'll withdraw more than 50% of the portfolio each year).

Morningstar's Christine Benz[14] offers some insights that show that mimicking RMDs helps to balance both portfolio valuations and longevity concerns. Unfortunately, this approach has downsides too. During the earliest years of retirement, the percentage of withdrawals is small. Retirees who want to spend more early in retirement while they are still physically healthy may not like the lower withdrawal percentage even if it ensures more optimal withdrawals over time.

---

13 "IRA Required Minimum Distribution Worksheet." IRS, https://www.irs.gov/pub/irs-tege/uniform_rmd_wksht.pdf.

14 Benz, Christine. "Should Your Withdrawals Mirror Your RMDs?" Morningstar, 7 March 2019, https://www.morningstar.com/articles/918416/should-your-withdrawals-mirror-your-rmds.

SPENDING FLOORS

The spending floor approach to withdrawals is a safety-first [15]approach to retirement planning. It emphasizes feeling comfortable with retirement spending while allowing retirees to manage an investment portfolio for discretionary expenses.

Retirees who want to use the spending floors approach need to understand their necessary expenditures and how much income they receive from guaranteed sources such as Social Security, pension income, and annuity income. This strategy recommends that retirees purchase enough guaranteed annuities to cover any gaps between their necessary expenditures and their guaranteed income sources.

However, there is no need to fully "pensionize" a retiree's full portfolio. Discretionary expenses may be funded through more aggressively invested investment portfolios. Retirees may opt to spend discretionary funds early or later in retirement as long as the portfolio allows continued expenditures.

Your financial independence number (FI number), as discussed in chapter 2, is a key indicator of success under the spending floors approach. This score divides necessary expenditures by "guaranteed" income in retirement.

---

15 Pechter, Kerry. "The Pfau Phenomenon." Retirement Income Journal, 10 October 2019, https://retirementincomejournal.com/article/the-pfau-phenomenon/. Accessed 3 August 2022.

NEVER TOUCHING THE PRINCIPAL

Retirees who are especially concerned with portfolio longevity and especially capital preservation may prefer a withdrawal strategy called "never touching the principal". Under this strategy, retirees spend dividends and interest from their portfolio, but they never sell underlying shares. If the portfolio appreciates in value, dividends and income should theoretically increase alongside the value of the portfolio.

This strategy is similar to the strategy of a real estate investor that only relies upon cash flow to fund their living expenses. The investor may spend cash flow from the rental income, but they do not plan to sell or put a mortgage on any of the investment properties. In this way, the underlying value of the real estate portfolio remains intact and future cash flow is more likely preserved.

While never touching the principal is a great way to maximize portfolio longevity, it means smaller expenditures, especially in the early years of retirement.

KEY TAKEAWAYS

We've covered seven of the most popular retirement withdrawal strategies. Each has been studied in-depth and could help retirees manage cash flow without worrying about a depleted portfolio. However, none of the strategies are foolproof. Each one could lead to financial difficulties due to market underperformance, inflation, or unexpected financial needs. The Retirement Budget Calculator may help you estimate these effects, but it does not cover every situation. It is designed with an emphasis on cash flow and is designed for those seeking a "can I afford to retire calculator".

Still, to maximize the likelihood of success, retirees will want to exercise discipline in adhering to their strategy. Retirees are more likely to have success by sticking with a strategy that matches their goals. If you're not sure which strategy works best for you, you may want to work with a fiduciary financial advisor who can help review your personal situation.

Chapter 8

INVESTING

BUCKETS OF MONEY: AN INVESTMENT STRATEGY FOR RETIREMENT PLANNING

During your career years, figuring out how to fund your lifestyle isn't too difficult. As long as you spend less than you earn, you're doing well. After decades of diligent saving and investing, new retirees face a new challenge. How to fund their lifestyle when their monthly income doesn't cover their expenses?

The buckets strategy is one investment framework designed to help answer that conundrum. This strategy breaks out investment strategies based on different time horizons. It provides for immediate financial needs while optimizing part of the portfolio for long-term growth. Here's what you need to know about it.

WHAT IS THE BUCKET STRATEGY?

As explained in the last chapter, the buckets strategy is a retirement framework that allows people to group investments based on timing. It helps retirees balance risk and reward over a longer time horizon (like a 30-year retirement window). Given the low-yield bond environment and the slow disappearance of private pensions, the buckets strategy can make a lot of sense for retirees. It can help retirees decide how much they can risk for growth, and how much money needs to be accessible. Even better, retirees can use the strategy to create a "retirement" paycheck. This monthly paycheck can be used to fund gaps in your retirement budget.

A simple version of the buckets strategy divides a retiree's financial assets into two buckets. The "cash" bucket would have money available in cash (savings accounts, CDs, or Money Market Funds) for short-term needs. The "investments" bucket includes investments such as stocks, bonds, and real estate.

In this very simplified strategy, a retiree can sell some of the investments (or take income from the investments) to fill the "cash" bucket. The retiree can then create a "retirement paycheck" by transferring cash to a checking account each month.

The buckets strategy offers several advantages for retirees. First, the large cash cushion allows a retiree to continue living their intended lifestyle even during a market downturn. Second, dividing assets into buckets allows a retiree to accept more volatility in the investments bucket. This can lead to higher growth prospects in the long run.

RECOMMENDED BUCKETS

Of course, simply knowing about two labels doesn't offer much guidance to retirees. Retirees (and aspiring retirees) can read up on the various ways to implement the strategy. But for simplicity, the Retirement Budget Calculator displays a four buckets strategy. These are the four buckets:

Income (also called cash):

This is money that you need in the short term, usually one to four years. Imagine a retiree with an annual spending of $50,000 per year. This person receives $35,000 from Social Security and other guaranteed income sources which leaves a gap of $15,000 per year. The income bucket would need to hold $15,000 to $60,000 in cash. The money should be accessible and not subject to risk. For example, it might be held in a Money Market Fund or a high yield bank account. While it can feel good to have a large cash cushion, don't overemphasize this bucket. Having too much cash can drag down portfolio performance. Money in the cash bucket should be separated from your primary checking account because cash in a primary account tends to be too easy to spend. Instead, retirees can set up automatic monthly transfers from the cash account to their checking account. This allows them to mimic the monthly paychecks they earned during their career.

Conservative:

The conservative bucket holds for four to six years from retirement. While it should be invested, its primary goal is to match inflation. Usually, high-quality government bonds or CDs would be appropriate for this bucket. A short-term or intermediate-term bond fund could work too. Given the low-yield environment, this bucket may just match inflation. It may even under-perform inflation slightly. However, in most cases, it will perform better than the cash bucket, and the assets should be fairly stable.

Intermediate:

In the intermediate bucket, retirees may want to take a bit more risk. This could be the right bucket for a mix of high-quality bonds and perhaps some equities depending on your willingness to accept volatility.

Growth:

The goal of this bucket is to produce long-term growth for your investment portfolio. Even if you're retired, a large proportion of your assets should be poised for growth. This is money you won't need for a decade or more. Most of this money should be invested in growth assets like stocks. The portion of your portfolio should ideally have both domestic and international exposure. Stock mutual funds or low-cost index funds could both fit well in this bucket. Preferred stock or higher-risk bonds may also fit in this bucket depending on your investment preferences.

HOW TO FILL YOUR BUCKETS DURING RETIREMENT

During retirement, you'll need to do some bucket maintenance. It would not make sense to spend all your conservative assets during the early years of retirement. Instead, retirees will want to refill the cash bucket using assets from the other buckets. Refilling buckets does not require rigid rule following or careful attention to the financial markets. Instead, a quick portfolio review a few times per year should be enough for a retiree to decide how to refill the buckets.

The exact refilling strategy can depend on market performance from the previous year or two. Since retirees start with enough cash to cover a few years of expenses, they should never be forced to sell assets that are "in the dumps."

To refill the cash bucket, retirees first want to look at income (dividends or yield) from all the buckets. If the income isn't sufficient to cover the full cash refill, investors may need to sell some portion of their assets to cover the gap.

When stocks do well, selling some of the stocks from the growth bucket is preferable. During a good year, the stock portfolio will continue to have a very high value, even after the retiree sells some shares. Of course, if stocks perform poorly, selling shares doesn't make sense. In that case, retirees may want to sell some of the bond assets from the conservative or moderate buckets.

When neither bonds nor stocks do well, retirees can hold off on rebalancing for a year or two. After all, the first bucket starts with enough cash to cover two or three years of spending. After a few years, it is likely that some part of the portfolio has recovered enough that retirees don't have to sell assets when the assets are at low prices. After all, the mantra "buy low, sell high" still applies during retirement.

Remember, every retirement investment strategy starts with your budget.

The buckets strategy is one useful framework for managing your investment portfolio during retirement. But this strategy, along with most other investing frameworks require you to know your budget. The Retirement Budget Calculator can help you understand your cash flow needs in a detailed way. It forces you to look in detail at your major budget categories, so you can successfully plan your total needs.

When you know and control your cash flow during retirement, any investing framework you choose is more likely to be a success.

THE ART AND SCIENCE OF INVESTING

"The stock market is a funny place. When one person sells and another person buys, they both think they are right." — Alan Greenspan

As we continue to look into academic research about investing, it is important to consider that the research is ever-evolving. As a result, our understanding and application are also evolving. Dimensional Fund Advisors has been at the forefront of taking academic research and creating mutual funds and exchange-traded funds that investors can use in their investment asset allocation. Vanguard has been a driver of market capitalization-weighted indexing and the driving force for bringing down fees for the average investor. Dimensional and Vanguard are two companies worth learning more about. At the end of the day, the name of the investing game is higher expected returns for a given level of risk.

It is important to consider the sources you are using for investment advice. Are you taking investment advice from main street,

Wall Street, or academia? Advice from main street would be the equivalent of listening to your friends, co-workers, or family members, who mean well but may not have spent the time to give appropriate advice for your specific situation. Wall Street advice is what I consider coming from brokerages, banks, and insurance companies and it can be tainted because there is often a sales motive and it can be hard to sort the research from the sales pitch. Academia on the other hand has a different motive. Academics are paid to research and teach. They have a different motive than main street or Wall Street. We are all gathering information all the time to help us understand how to optimize our investing strategy. This area of financial science from the academic community is always evolving, and as we gather the information, we must decide who is a trustworthy source of the information we will use to make important decisions. If you must choose between these three sources of information, I'd recommend you start with academic research.

Two different philosophies can be combined for how you can invest your money in the stock market. Tactical investment management, which I call the "art of investing", and Strategic Asset Allocation, which I call the "science of investing" are those philosophies.

We'll take a look at each of these below. I believe that both of these styles can be good for different reasons. I tell our clients tactical and strategic investment styles serve a purpose, and depending on market conditions and your goals, different strategies may be better suited than others.

Tactical Investing

In Tactical or Active Investment Money Management, the managers are seeking opportunities and looking to avoid risk by actively trading and managing a portfolio, which means they will at times move your investments out of the stock market and into cash. This style of management, the art side of investing, can't be academically or scientifically proven, but some managers have had very impressive results over a long period. Even though no guarantees exist that these results will continue, you would be hard-pressed to discount what some of the tactical money managers have achieved. The reason you would consider tactical investing in retirement is to attempt to reduce volatility for a segment of your investing strategy.

Strategic Investing

Strategic Asset Allocation was born through the "Modern Portfolio Theory".[16] Harry Markowitz won the Nobel Prize in 1990 for developing this theory. Willam Sharpe won the Nobel Prize the same year for his contributions to the Capital Asset Pricing Model[17], which we'll talk more about soon. Then in October 2013, a man named Eugene Fama won the Nobel prize for the Efficient-

---

16 "Modern Portfolio Theory (MPT) Definition." Investopedia, https://www.investopedia.com/terms/m/modernportfoliotheory.asp.

17 "Explaining The Capital Asset Pricing Model (CAPM)." Investopedia, https://www.investopedia.com/articles/06/capm.asp.

Market Hypothesis[18], which is often associated with the Modern Portfolio Theory. The Efficient-Market Hypothesis asserts how the financial markets are informationally efficient, and one cannot consistently predict returns in excess of average market returns.

"Investing is not nearly as difficult as it looks. Successful investing involves doing a few things right and avoiding serious mistakes."
– John C. Bogle aka Jack Bogle, the founder of Vanguard.

The Modern Portfolio Theory proposes how rational investors will use diversification to optimize their portfolios and decide how a risk asset should be priced. Modern Portfolio Theory assumes that investors are risk-averse, meaning that given two assets that offer the same expected return investors will prefer the less risky one. Thus, an investor will take on increased risk only if compensated by higher expected returns. Conversely, an investor who wants higher returns must accept more risk. The precise trade-off will differ depending on the investor's individual risk aversion characteristics. The conclusion is that a reasonable investor would not put money into a portfolio if another one with a better risk-return profile already exists. If an alternative portfolio with a better-anticipated return exists for that level of risk, the rational investor will select it.

---

18 Downey, Lucas. "Efficient-Market Hypothesis (EMH) Definition." Investopedia, https://www.investopedia.com/terms/e/efficientmarkethypothesis.asp. Accessed 3 August 2022.

A landmark study by Brinson, Hood, Beebower (BHB)[19] conducted in 1986, updated in 1991 and expanded in 1993, suggests that portfolio asset allocation is the most important long-term determinant of investment results. Strategic asset allocation also suggests that no one can accurately and consistently predict when shifts in market leadership will occur or how long they will last. The market leaders of one year, are often the laggards of the next. Strategic asset allocation, therefore, suggests that it's important to spread your assets across multiple investment asset classes and sectors so you can potentially benefit from an upswing in any one asset class. It also suggests that the stock market is efficient and that all asset classes do not usually move in tandem. We're hoping that when one asset class zigs, the other zags because we're searching for a balance between these asset classes.

Rebalancing Inside of Strategic Asset Allocation

Have you ever heard that the secret to success in the stock market is to buy low and sell high? Unfortunately, many studies point out that individual investors are fairly bad at timing the stock market. These studies suggest that most people tend to invest after a long and sustained bull market and then they sell after the market has crashed. Essentially they're buying high and selling low. What if a way existed to strategically buy low and sell high? One of the ways I believe you can intelligently invest in the stock market is to create a broadly diversified portfolio across asset classes (equities,

---

19 "Determinants of Portfolio Performance: Financial Analysts Journal: Vol 42, No 4." Taylor & Francis Online, 31 December 2018, https://www.tandfonline.com/doi/abs/10.2469/faj.v42.n4.39.

fixed income such as bonds, cash equivalents and commodities) and sectors (agriculture, commerce, tech, health services, etc.) across the globe. This method of diversification is called Strategic Asset Allocation and is built by using low-cost index mutual funds or exchange-traded funds (ETFs).

A powerful ingredient that makes Strategic Asset Allocation attractive is rebalancing the portfolio. Rebalancing is counterintuitive because it forces you to sell some of your winners and buy more of your losers. If you agree that the market is efficient, then you agree that no one asset class or sector will ever dominate from year-to-year and that eventually, a regression to the mean will occur. So, while large-cap growth may be the best asset class this year, perhaps small-cap value will be the best next year and treasury inflation-protected securities the next. Rebalancing is an intelligent, non-emotional way to buy low and sell high. How often you should rebalance your portfolio can and should be debated, especially depending on what stage of life you're in and the tax considerations of your portfolio. If you're in accumulation mode versus distribution mode, some people will rebalance a portfolio based on a calendar year of historical data. An old saying goes, "sell in May and go away". But instead of selling, you could use this historical data to rebalance your portfolio in May. Depending on whether you have your money invested in a qualified or non-qualified account may impact how often you want to rebalance your portfolio from a tax planning standpoint. We set drift parameters for our strategic portfolios at anywhere from 2% to 5%. Any time one asset class has drifted out of alignment by more than 2% or 5%, that's an indicator for us to rebalance a portfolio.

Rebalancing as a part of a Strategic Asset Allocation is a calculated, non-emotional way of helping you buy low and sell high. Many academic articles have been written on Modern Portfolio Theory, Efficient-Market Hypothesis, and the benefits of Strategic Asset Allocation and rebalancing.

Both strategic and tactical investment styles offer advantages and disadvantages. Market conditions will determine which one of these styles will perform the best. In an upward trending market like we had from the early 1980s through 1999, Strategic Asset Allocation will probably have performed best. In a very volatile market, as we had in 2008 or March of 2020, tactical asset allocation may have performed better.

WHY INCLUDE TACTICAL POSITIONS?

I want to address questions that many people have about Active Money Management or Tactical Money Management. Why would you want to include the tactical position and include what I call the "art of investing"? Aren't you going to pay more money in fees and expect a lower return? Keep in mind that investing in retirement is different from your accumulation years. When you're accumulating wealth, volatility is just noise. Let me say that again. When you're accumulating wealth, volatility is just noise. If anything, the volatility helps you. Hopefully, you're making regular contributions to your retirement accounts and by doing so you're dollar-cost averaging those contributions. You're buying more shares at lower prices and so, volatility helps you accumulate wealth. However, the exact opposite happens in the distribution phase of your financial life.

If you're selling shares to generate income while the market is falling in value, you are reverse dollar-cost averaging. So then why might you want to include a tactical position? The reason you would include it is to help reduce volatility in the portfolio. You would not do it for lower fees, nor would you do it for higher expected returns. You would include tactical money management to help reduce volatility at a time where volatility is no longer noise, but real risk that could impact you negatively as you draw money out of your investments. Adding Active Money Management is no guarantee that you will reduce volatility. You would want to review the long-term track record of any tactical managers before investing and make sure that you're willing to pay the higher fees and accept the fact that there's probably going to be a lower performance for the expectation that there would be reduced volatility.

If you have more than five years before retirement, you don't need to worry about adding Tactical MoneyManagement, unless you tend to be more conservative. If you are in your 20s, 30s, and 40s, I would recommend that you just invest in Strategic Asset Allocation. In my years of experience, I've never had someone walk into my office and when I ask them what the purpose of their money is and have them they say, "Jason, the purpose of my money is to beat the market or beat an index." They've never even said, "The purpose of my money is to track an index." Most of the time, what they say is they just want their money to earn a fair rate of return, maybe a few points above inflation, and they don't want to worry about running out of money in retirement. Additionally, when things go really bad, they don't want to get wiped out in retirement.

The other day I read an article about people who were investing in leveraged funds. In a matter of weeks, they saw most of their wealth wiped out because they were playing a high-risk game, which is not the game you want to be playing as you start transitioning into retirement. As an advisor, I find that I spend a lot of time keeping our clients from investing in ways they don't need to in this phase of their lives.

ARE THERE DOWNSIDES TO STRATEGIC ASSET ALLOCATION?

Let's talk about some of the negatives associated with Strategic Asset Allocation. Markowitz (referenced earlier with Modern Portfolio Theory) stated, "We're trying to minimize risk for a given return." So how do you do that? He says the answer is to diversify. Don't put all of your eggs in one basket. Sharpe (also referenced earlier with the Capital Asset Pricing Model or CAPM) explains that CAPM has to do with the price of a security, its risks, and its expected return. He says there are two key takeaways from CAPM.

First, he says the most efficient strategy is to be broadly diversified. Second, he essentially tells us that there is the potential for greater reward for those who take the greater risk. He says there will be a reward with higher expected returns for bearing the risks of doing badly in bad times. It's very important to understand that life is risky. It's so risky that none of us are getting out of here alive.

If you think that you can create a strategy and not accept any risk, then you're going to have to accept that there's not going to be a significant return. There's a trade-off. Accepting that life is risky is just understanding that this is the world we live in. And that's a good thing. We get compensated for the risk we take.

What most people have come to learn from all of this academic research is to use index funds for broad diversification, keep your fees low, and use a long-term strategy for accumulating wealth by following something like the Modern Portfolio Theory.

But what about the next phase as you transition out of wealth accumulation and into the distribution phase of investing? Let's revisit what our referenced Nobel Prize winners in economics have told us. We have all of this academic theory around portfolio construction, but it was all based on the accumulation of assets while we were still working.

After Markowitz won the Nobel Prize in Economics, he was asked to contribute an article to a magazine called the Financial Services Review about the implications of Modern Portfolio Theory for the individual investor. This was back in 1991, which was one year after he had won the Nobel Prize for the same theory. In this article, he writes, "But an evening of reflection convinced me that there were clear differences in the central features of investments for institutions and investments for individuals."

He goes on to say, "As I thought about the subject further on subsequent days, I found myself of two minds." He says that when he wrote the dissertation that ultimately won him the Nobel Prize, "The investing institution, which I had most in my mind when developing portfolio theory for my dissertation, was the open-end investment company or mutual fund."

Modern Portfolio Theory was based on investments for institutions not necessarily for individuals and Wade Pfau points out that the theory doesn't account for any need to take distributions from those investments.

In Pfau's book, *Safety-First Retirement Planning*[20], he explains it this way (this is the key to understanding how the retirement income problem differs from the Modern Portfolio Theory approach), "Households must meet spending goals over an unknown length of time in retirement. Modern Portfolio Theory just seeks to grow wealth over a single time period, such as a year when there is no need to take distributions from the portfolio. It's an assets-only model."

In a model where distributions and time are not important, Modern Portfolio Theory is a winning strategy. This is why it works so well for people who are in the accumulation years. However, it may not work as well when you're in the retirement phase of life when you're pulling funds from your portfolio instead of accumulating funds.

Modern Portfolio Theory and Capital Asset Pricing Model are all geared towards accumulating wealth. Oftentimes I meet with people who have been using these strategies during the accumulation phase of life, and they've been very pleased- but the game changes in retirement. Now time and distributions are factors that need to be considered. Managing volatility, standard

---

20 Pfau, Wade Donald. Safety-First Retirement Planning: An Integrated Approach for a
    Worry-Free Retirement. Retirement Researcher Media, 2019.

deviation, sequence of returns, and cash flow from investments become the new goal.

You're no longer in the wealth accumulation phase of life. When you retire, you want your money to continue to work, but it needs to work differently. We know that the future is unknown and unknowable. The longer I work in the investment field, the more humility becomes an important virtue. Making decisions based on past performance is like driving your car and only looking in the rearview mirror. You might get where you're going, but I wouldn't want to be the passenger in the car.

I like how Markowitz thinks about financial planning. In a paper that he wrote back in 1991, he used the term "The Game of Life model", where he says, "Time and uncertainty are the heart of the problem". If you think about it, the Game of Life model that he talks about creating is a computer program that would allow you to test your hypothesis.

As we near or start retirement, we need a way to test which investment theory will work best for us. And that's what I built in the Retirement Budget Calculator. If you think you can retire, why not test your own Game of Life model and see if it's going to work.

WHAT CAN YOU DO TO CREATE A GUARANTEED INCOME STREAM?

Now we can discuss Sharpe. He also won the Nobel Prize back in 1990 for this Capital Asset Pricing Model (CAPM). Not only is Sharpe a Nobel Prize-winning economist, but he is also a professor of finance emeritus for Stanford University graduate school of business. In 2019, he was 85 years old and was interviewed by Barron's. The resulting article is titled, How To Secure Lasting Retirement Income. Let me share with you a few quotes from this article. "The most difficult problem in finance," says Sharpe, "is knowing how to strike a balance between having enough income to meet your current needs and having enough to get you through your lifetime."

He goes on to say, (and this is key for you accumulators that are trying to make the switch to retirement and distribution), "Over the course of my career, I have always been interested in individual investors. My earlier work focused on helping people accumulate money." Again, Modern Portfolio Theory, Efficient-Market Hypothesis, and Capital Asset Pricing Model are all geared towards this accumulation phase. The idea of broad diversification works well in a strategy where time and distributions aren't important. He also says, "If you invest your money in almost anything, except in an annuity with a cost of living adjustment, you're going to be subject to two kinds of uncertainty. Investment uncertainty and mortality uncertainty."

I like this. He goes on to say, "When you retire and make your initial decision on buying annuities, investing, and adopting some sort of spending plan, I would think it would make sense to sit down at least once at the outset with a financial advisor". One of the things that he knows is that if you keep your fees low, you're going to do better. He adds, "I don't necessarily advocate paying 1% of your assets to an advisor indefinitely".

For some of you, it's a really good plan to hire an advisor and pay 1% per year in fees. On the other hand, some of you are well-equipped. This is an area where you spend a lot of time and paying the 1% fee may not make sense. And for somebody like Sharpe, who spent his whole life in this field of finance and investing, it may not make sense for him. But the one point I would argue is that for many of you, this is not how you spend all of your time, nor is it where you want to spend all of your time.

You've done a really good job in terms of accumulating money because you've been a good saver. You've kept your spending low. But paying a fee to get the advice makes sense for you. And so if that's the case, some things are worth outsourcing. We will look at hiring an advisor and the costs and benefits of doing so in a future chapter.

Let's take a look at another quote from this article in Barron's. Sharpe says, "We who have been on the investment side, have been babbling about pooling investment risk all our lives. Diversify, diversify, diversify. And yet when we retire, longevity risk is at least as big a risk as investment risk. And you really should consider pooling some of that particularly as you get into the later stages of retirement." When he's talking about pooling longevity risk and mortality risk, he's talking about considering buying an annuity to create a floor of guaranteed income for some basic level of spending.

Still referencing this article that is from 2019, the interviewer says, "Your e-book outlines a strategy that you call a lockbox. Can you take us through it?" To this Sharpe responds, "The idea is that you segment your money. It's similar to using buckets, but with a time component."

One of the things that I've been preaching for years now is that time is the cure to the volatility of the stock market. The more time you have, the more risk you can afford to take. But what I love about Sharpe's work when it comes to time segmentation, bucketing, laddering your money over time, or lockboxes as he likes to call them, is listening to what he says next. He says, "The bottom line is that bucketing your assets in annual increments with different initial asset mixes in these lockboxes can provide a more efficient production of retirement income over time."

In the Retirement Budget Calculator, we show you how to diversify using time segments for your specific situation that is based on the gap between your guaranteed income and your projected spending.

We've had guests on our podcast, *Sound Retirement Planning*[21], in the past that say by using buckets, "Well, it reduces your overall return by having different buckets." But Sharpe says it can provide more efficient production of retirement income over time. Remember, you have to ask yourself as you're making this transition into retirement, "What's the purpose of the money?" Are you still in the accumulation phase of life or have you made the transition into the distribution phase?

---

21 Sound Retirement Planning - A Retirement Plan Designed To Help You Achieve Clarity, Confidence & Freedom, https://soundretirementplanning.com/.

You've got to think differently about your money as you transition into retirement. A challenge you will run into is that a large group of practitioner advisors like and recommend buckets and another segment of advisors prefer to use a different withdrawal strategy, and they do not recommend the use of buckets. Ultimately you will have to evaluate the information and decide what is best for you.

SO WHERE DOES THIS LEAVE US?

Should you consider a Tactical Investment Strategy as part of your plan to help reduce standard deviation or volatility? Yes, because the sequence of returns risk is real. Now it doesn't mean everybody's going to want to pay the higher fee and that's okay. But should you consider it? Well, I think so.

Should you include Strategic Asset Allocation as part of your overall investment strategy? When you have enough time on your side, I would say so. Remember, Modern Portfolio Theory, Efficient-Market Hypothesis, and Capital Asset Pricing Models work great in an asset-only strategy, but now we're not talking about asset-only. We're not talking about accumulation. We're talking about distribution. We're talking about a time when time matters. Should you use buckets, or (as Sharpe calls them) "lockboxes" to diversify your money across time as you head into retirement? Well, I think so. That's what we've been talking about for the last several years on the Sound Retirement Radio podcast. I would argue yes. And it's not just because I am a financial advisor who walks life with real people that have been on this journey, but it's because this is what some in the academic community also recommend as a way of dealing with, as Sharpe says, "The most difficult problem in finance".

Should you consider purchasing an annuity with some of your retirement funds to provide a guaranteed income at a point in the future, and as a way to de-risk as you head into retirement? Should you create a floor? Do you need one? Well, I don't know because I don't know your situation. Some of you already have a good floor. Sometimes the floor that Social Security creates for you is enough. But for some of you, you really should have an additional annuity income. Some of you have a pension, which is an annuity, and that creates the floor that you need.

In the Retirement Budget Calculator, we created the Secure Income Score to determine how much of your essential expenses are covered by guaranteed income, and we made the benchmark 80%. If you have 80% of your essential expenses covered by guaranteed income, then you do not need to consider purchasing an annuity.

Some of you don't have pensions or Social Security, and so you need to be thinking about taking some of your retirement assets and saying, "How much do I need to annuitize to guarantee income?" An annuity is the only financial tool you can use with the words "guaranteed income". Of course the guarantees are based on the financial strength of the company, but to guarantee at least a basic standard of living is wise. I heard somebody once call it his beer and pizza money. He says he doesn't want to gamble his beer and pizza money. I think maybe beer and pizza would fall under more discretionary spending in my opinion, but you do want to be able to keep the lights on. You want to be able to pay the mortgage if you have one. You want to be able to buy food and groceries.

Chapter 9

WHY ASSET ALLOCATION IS SO IMPORTANT

As I've met with people around the country, I've found that many people don't have an asset allocation strategy. Many people have only made investments in various stocks, bonds, and mutual funds with no real guidance on portfolio construction or asset allocation. They just know that they should have some money in stocks, some money in bonds, and some cash, which is a very basic understanding of asset allocation. Let's explore why the subject is so much more important than just that simple structure.

Risk is different once you retire as you're no longer saving and accumulating, and as I've said before, during that time, risk was just noise. But if anything, volatility helps you accumulate wealth because when you're making regular contributions and dollar-cost averaging into the market. Volatility allows you to buy during the dip.

I've heard the analogy that investing is like climbing Mount Everest. Climbing Mount Everest would be like the accumulation phase, whereas the distribution phase would be like coming back down from the peak.. An interesting statistic is that more people die coming down Mount Everest than going up. An article in Scientific American said that only about 15% of deaths occur from attempting to scale Mount Everest, whereas 56% of the deaths occur on the way down. The analogy helps us understand that sometimes the way down, or the distribution phase, can be more important and risky than the way up or the accumulation phase.

Let's look at the distribution of wealth, which is different from how most people think. Many of the investment podcasts that I listen to are focused on the accumulation of wealth while only a few talk about portfolio distributions or how asset allocation is applied in the distribution phase of retirement. Let's start with answering one of the most basic questions: What is asset allocation? Asset allocation is balancing risk and reward by investing in different asset classes with the expectation that they do not all move in tandem. It's finding the sweet spot on the efficient frontier that maximizes returns for a given level of risk.

An overly simplistic example of asset allocation would be to determine how much to hold in cash, bonds, and stocks. Asset allocation, even more simply means not having all of your eggs in one basket. To create an asset allocation strategy, you would want to understand what rate of return is required to meet your future cash flow needs. You will also want to know how different asset classes have performed historically. Lastly you're going to want to make some forward-looking assumptions about how the asset classes will perform in the future.

ASSET CLASS DIVERSIFICATION

Now that we have an idea of how to define asset allocation, why do we say it is important in the first place? Well, this all started back in 1986 with the BHB study we mentioned in Chapter 8. In that study, they concluded that asset allocation explained 93.6% of the variation in a portfolio's quarterly returns, while stock picking and market timing played minor roles. Some of the more recent discussions around this early work are that its focus was on the variability of returns, not on return levels or relative performance, which is what most investors are interested in. It's the academic community that has informed our understanding of the importance of asset allocation.

It is also important to take a moment to talk about diversification because that's another word that gets used regularly, but I think of diversification differently than I think of asset allocation.

Especially in a retirement portfolio, I define diversification as a withdrawal strategy over time & risk levels. Essentially diversifying your investments for retirement cash flow planning, assuming that cash flow planning is the process of identifying future income, expenses, and major expenditures so that they are coordinated with investment planning.

The first step is to diversify the time horizon based on when you're going to need the money. Then, depending on how long before you need access to the investments, we'd determine how much risk you should take for each time segment. Once we know how much you plan to spend, we can create each time segment.

We would then create an asset allocation strategy to match up with each of those time segments. The segments needed in the early years would be invested more conservatively, while the segments that are needed in the later years would be invested more aggressively. This concept seems fairly easy to understand, and from my experience, a lot of people like the idea. They think it makes sense.

Now that we know what asset allocation is, and why it's important to look at it, let's look at how this applies to you, as you shift from making the transition from the accumulation phase of asset allocation into the distribution phase of asset allocation.

In the next few paragraphs, I am going to discuss the Callan Periodic Table of Investment Returns[22]. It might be easier to follow along if you do an internet search for Callan Periodic Table so that you can view the chart. I'm going to do my best to describe to you what I'm looking at, but if you'll imagine a spreadsheet or a grid, or a table, if you will, along the top of the spreadsheet are columns. And each column represents a year starting with the year 2000 and going through the year 2019 (although this chart is updated yearly). In each row of the columns are colorful little boxes and each of these boxes represents an asset class and how it performed for that year. Each asset class has been assigned a color so it can be tracked more easily visually across the years.

The asset classes being represented are as follows:

- Real Estate

- US Fixed Income

---

22 Kloepfer, Jay. "Periodic Table." Callan, https://www.callan.com/periodic-table/.

- Cash

- Small-Cap Equity

- Global Fixed Income, excluding the United States

- High Yield

- Large-Cap Equity

- International Developed, excluding the United States

- Emerging Markets

This colorful table illustrates that no one asset class is consistently the top or the bottom performer. But, if you're like me, what you try to do is recognize patterns. And, and you think to yourself, "Boy, if I could just identify the asset class that's consistently at the top, wouldn't that be a winning strategy?" Or maybe just avoid the asset classes that are consistently at the bottom. I think the chart does a pretty good job of showing you why trying to play that game is not going to get you very far.

Here are a couple of things that I noticed as I looked at the top and bottom performers over this period from 2000 to 2019.

At the very top, the asset classes that consistently showed up the most include

- Real estate (the best performer), which showed up five times out of the last 20 years.

- Emerging Markets also showed up five times

- US Fixed Income showed up three times, as did small-cap equity

- Large-cap equity was in the top spot twice

- Global Fixed Income and Cash were each in that top spot once.

As I look at the bottom performers over this period

- Cash was the very worst performer eight times over this 20-year period

- Emerging Markets was there four times

- Global Fixed Income and Developed International, excluding the United States were both there twice

- Large-Cap Equity, US Fixed Income, and Real Estate were all there once

The real power of looking at the Callan Periodic Table of Investment Returns helps you to understand that it's going to be a really tough game if you think you're always going to pick the best-performing asset class each year. What it encourages you to consider is that instead of trying to just pick the best performer, wouldn't it be more advantageous to broadly diversify your holdings across all of the different classes and then rebalance?

Rebalancing, as discussed previous, forces you to sell some of the positions that have done well in the good years and buy more of the positions that have done poorly. It's counterintuitive. It forces you to think differently about the market. It forces you to think differently than the way that most people want to think. People want to hold onto their winners and sell their losers, and when you rebalance a portfolio it's forcing you to do the exact opposite of that.

It's important to understand that we're talking about asset allocation for people who are transitioning into retirement. The advice that people who are accumulating wealth will be given is likely not the same as for people who are making the transition into the distribution or retirement phase. What got you here might not get you there.

In the analogy about climbing Mount Everest, while there is certainly a risk, the accumulation phase doesn't feel as daunting when you have a job and you have income coming in. But suddenly you're heading back down that mountain, and now what you've saved is what you've saved. You have to make that money last for the rest of your life. That is not a time to be experimenting with what you think is going to work. You have to have a good, disciplined strategy. Keep your fees as low as possible. Choose the asset allocation that is going to work for you, and diversify your money across time segments. That's what I would encourage you to consider.

So here are a few questions that I think are worth asking yourself as you began to make this transition:

- Why did you select your current asset allocation strategy?

- What was the methodology used for creating your asset allocation strategy?

- Was there a methodology?

- Is your asset allocation strategy designed for an accumulation strategy or is it designed for a distribution strategy?

- What did you design it for?

FACTORS

One of Fama's most significant contributions to investing has come from his collaboration with his colleague Kenneth French and their work in the development of Factor Models for Investing and their contribution to portfolio construction at Dimensional Fund Advisors[23]. Asset allocation models based on a factor-based framework have become incredibly popular in the investment community, and many investors are wondering whether or not they should incorporate factors into their retirement investment framework.

Who are Eugene Fama and Kenneth French?

Fama is an American economist who is currently a professor at the University of Chicago Booth School of Business. Fama is best known for his work on asset pricing and portfolio management. French is an American economist who is currently a professor at

---

23 "Fama-French Three-Factor Model - Components, Formula & Uses." Corporate Finance Institute, 18 February 2022, https://corporatefinanceinstitute.com/resources/ knowledge/finance/fama-french-three-factor-model/.

Dartmouth College. French is best known for his work on factor models, asset allocation, and mutual fund performance. Fama and French rank within the top 10 most cited fellows of the American Finance Association, recognized for their work in financial science. Both Fama and French are on the board of directors at Dimensional Fund Advisors.

What is Factor Research?

Factor research is a way to organize historical data to try and understand what drives differences in returns across different groups of securities. From this research and these models, you can glean insights about drivers of expected returns and differences in risk across different asset categories.

What are the Factors?

The three original factors are

- market risk,

- size risk, and

- value risk.

Market risk is the risk that cannot be diversified away. Size risk is the risk associated with small-capitalization stocks. Value risk is the risk associated with stocks that are trading at a low price-to-earnings ratio or low price-to-book ratio. Factors such as momentum, profitability, and investment have also been identified.

Small Companies Have Higher Expected Returns than Large Large Companies

In the early 1980's, David Booth who had completed his MBA at the University of Chicago and who had been a student of Fama, identified that there were not many strategies that targeted the returns of small-cap stocks. There was evidence at the time that smaller cap stocks had higher average returns historically than large-cap stocks and the expectations were that there would be higher expected returns going forward. So Booth – the co-founder of Dimensional - created the Dimensional US Micro Cap Portfolio, arguably the first systematic factor-based investment strategy for institutional investors. The strategy focused on small-cap stocks, which have historically outperformed their counterpart, large-cap stocks.

Value Over Growth or Low Price = Higher Expected Returns

Another factor includes a company's value, which can be derived from a company's financial statements. These can include a company's market price, which is determined by looking at price-to-book ratio, price-to-earnings ratio, dividends, and free cash flow. Generally, companies are categorized as being either growth or value. Growth companies tend to have a higher price-to-earnings ratio, have a greater focus on reinvesting earnings into assets, and don't usually pay dividends. Value companies tend to have lower price-to-earnings ratios, with less of a focus on asset growth, and pay dividends. Value stocks have historically outperformed growth stocks, however, there have been extended periods where growth stocks have outperformed value.

Investment Returns

Factor Investing takes into consideration, at a given price, how much in expected return an investor can expect, given a company's cash flow and profitability. Research done by Dimensional has shown that companies with larger investments - or asset growth of their balance sheets – tend to decrease expected returns for investors, as compared to companies with smaller investments. Historically, businesses with high asset growth or investment have had lower returns than businesses with lower asset growth. As such, Dimensional has explored strategies that take into account the asset growth of companies, finding that excluding small high-asset-growth firms has resulted in increased value in portfolio strategy.

An example can be found in a simulation run by Dimensional, which explored the impact of excluding firms with high asset growth in the small-cap market, using data from the US small-cap market from 1974 to 2018. What they found was that excluding growth firms with low profitability and high investment resulted in a return of 14.49%, as compared to the overall small-cap market, which returned 12.65%. A similar pattern was observed in international markets, as well as emerging markets, all of which had experienced greater returns with the exclusion of small, high asset growth firms and low profitability growth companies.

Profitability Premium

In addition, a business's profitability is another key factor when investing. Given the extensive amount of research on using profitability to increase expected returns, investors need to take notice of this factor when making investment decisions. Professors Fama and French are credited with taking financial data that is observable and using it to find information about expected future profitability for companies. Their research showed that a business's current profitability can tell us about its profitability for years to come, thereby helping predict the success of a company's stock – or the investor's expected return - in the long run.

Building off of Fama and French's influential findings, Professor Robert Novy-Marx[24], a world-renowned expert on empirical asset pricing, explored the relationship between different measures of current profitability to stock returns. An important insight that Novy-Marx found was that in taking a company's profits, not all current revenues and expenses have information about future profits. He found that firms sometimes have revenues or expenses that are "extraordinary", which they don't expect to recur. Accounting for these anomalies, Novy-Marx utilized national data from the 1960s to 2013 that excluded non-recurring expenses or revenue and revealed a strong connection between current profitability and future stock returns. He discovered that firms with better profitability had higher returns than those with less.

Research by Dimensional further confirmed Novy-Marx's work. Data taken from Dimensional High vs. Low Profitability Indices have shown that from 1964 to 2016, the High Profitability Index had annual compound returns of 12.55%, as

---

24 "The Other Side of Value: The Gross Profitability Premium - Robert Novy-MarxŽ June, 2012." Robert Novy-Marx, http://rnm.simon.rochester.edu/research/OSoV.pdf. Accessed 5 August 2022.

compared to 8.23% for the Low Profitability Index. The same pattern was found in International Markets, as well as in emerging markets with high profitability firms outperforming low profitability firms.

In conclusion, investing doesn't have to be a guessing game, and rational decisions can be made, backed by data and research done by those in the academic community. You can't expect that picking individual stocks will generate superior returns. Broad diversification in an intelligent way to reduce risks when investing and insights from the academic community show that developing investment portfolios based on financial science can yield the desired results for the individual investor seeking higher expected risk-adjusted returns. Looking at factors such as size, value, investment, and profitability have shown to be important and reliable drivers of higher expected returns.

Vanguard offers low-cost market-cap-weighted index funds and Dimensional offers what I would call enhanced index funds that incorporate financial science to tilt portfolios with higher expected returns by using factors. You can combine both Vanguard and Dimensional funds to enjoy low costs, broad diversification, and academic research to increase confidence in your retirement investment strategy.

Chapter 10

REBALANCE OR BUY LOW, SELL HIGH

A sailor navigating stormy seas is analogous to a trader in the financial market. You may have heard this saying "a pessimist complains about the wind, the optimist expects it to change, and the realist adjusts the sails." When it comes to investing, adjusting the sails is what I call rebalancing. Before we take a more in depth look at rebalancing, we will look at stock performance. Everyone wants to buy a stock at a low price and sell it at a high price. However, a research paper by JP Morgan Asset Management titled *The Agony and Ecstasy*,[25] published in 2014, looked at the risks and rewards of concentrated stock positions compared with the performance of the overall Russell 3000 index from the year 1980 through 2014.

The Russell 3000 index measures the performance of the largest 3000 US companies representing approximately 98% of the investible US equity market. It's reconstituted annually to ensure that new and growing companies are reflected. The researchers

---

25 Morgan, JP. "Eotm the agony and the ecstasy." J.P. Morgan Private Bank, https:// privatebank.jpmorgan.com/content/dam/jpm-wm-aem/global/pb/en/insights/eye-on-the-market/eotm-the-agony-and-the-ecstasy.pdf.

analyzed all the stocks that were part of the Russell 3000 index from 1980 to 2014, which included a database of 13,000 large, mid, and small-cap stocks and there were a few important takeaways that are summarized in the executive summary of this report. Some companies substantially outperform their broad market and maintain their value.

However, the odds have been stacked against their average concentrated holder. According to "The Agony and Ecstasy" article, "The risk of permanent impairment using the universe of Russell 3000 companies since 1980, shows roughly 40% of all stocks have suffered a permanent 70% decline from their peak value." It also states, "40% of stocks experience negative lifetime returns versus the broad market. The return on the median stocks since its inception versus an investment in the Russell 3000 index was negative 54%, two-thirds of all stocks underperformed the Russell 3000 index, and for 40% of all stocks, their absolute returns were negative."

This paper states that since 1980, over 320 companies were deleted from the S&P 500 for business distress reasons. We think that it's almost un-American for a company to go out of business, but the reality is that companies go out of business all the time. According to Statista the average lifespan of a company on the S&P 500 index is only 21 years.

This is true even for the big companies, the strong companies, the companies that are big enough to make it into an index like the Russell 3000 or the S&P 500 index. Bogle is quoted as saying, "Don't look for the needle in the haystack, just buy the haystack."

This JP Morgan study reveals that 40% of companies suffered a permanent decline of 70% and two-thirds of companies do not perform as well as the index and only 7% of the companies outperformed the index averages. You can see how stock picking is like trying to find the needle in the haystack. This study shows you that stock picking comes with a high degree of risk and that there are few reasons to believe it will work.

Diversification can help you achieve the returns you need without taking on significant risks. Instead of attempting to discover the next big winning stock, you can benefit from diversification by investing in a low-cost index fund. Trying to be the next Warren Buffet with stock picking may be fun when you're accumulating wealth and you don't need to depend on the resources, but if you're getting ready to transition into retirement, consider using low-cost index funds to create broad diversification across asset classes, sectors, and to be diversified across the entire globe.

INVESTMENT PORTFOLIO CONSTRUCTION

Portfolio construction means that you're going to need to make some decisions about how to allocate your investments across several different dimensions. How much will you have in domestic stock versus international? Will you include emerging markets? How will you allocate between value and growth? Will you overweight technology or consumer staples, or how about companies that pay dividends versus companies that don't? What type of fixed income will you include? What about high yield? How about the duration of those bond holdings? What will you be comfortable with? Will you include fixed income alternatives, such as certificates of deposit or fixed annuities, or savings accounts? How will you diversify across taxable tax-deferred and tax-free positions?

You can use index funds to make the asset allocation decisions, but at some point, the rubber will hit the road and you will have to decide on how you're going to construct the portfolio. Just like taking concentrated stock positions is hard to justify, it is also hard to justify taking concentrated asset allocation decisions when you can easily enjoy broad global diversification. Often people look at the historical performance of an asset class to try to understand the risks associated with the asset allocation mix and then construct an investment portfolio that will have the qualities, characteristics, risk profile, and performance that it needs to make sure that you're going to be okay in retirement.

WHAT IS REBALANCING AND HOW IS IT IMPLEMENTED?

The idea of rebalancing is to maintain asset allocation over time. If you don't rebalance, then the investments that perform better tend to overtake all your asset allocation strategies. For example, let's say in 1990, you decided to invest 60% in stocks and 40% in bonds because you were comfortable with the risk-reward of this type of asset allocation. If you never rebalanced from 1990 to 2020, then your stock allocation would've grown from 60% to 81% by the year 2020. And the bonds would only represent about 19%. Typically, you have the bonds in the portfolio for that ballast for stability. You're not trying to earn a lot of money as it is. You're just trying to remove some of the risks of the stock segment of your portfolio.

Now, 30 years later, you would have much more exposure to stocks than you had originally decided upon, which historically has meant being more aggressive and taking on more risk, and accepting higher volatility.

Rebalancing is the process of realigning the weightings of portfolio assets. For example, if the original asset mix was 60% stock, and 40% bond based on your risk profile and the projected returns needed to support your retirement cash flow, then you would want to maintain that weighting over time. Rebalancing can also mean rebalancing within the 60% stock allocation. You can rebalance across asset classes, such as large, mid, small-cap, domestic, international, and emerging markets, and rebalance within the bonds across duration and credit quality.

I would say to anyone who wants to manage risk, that the purpose of rebalancing is more about managing risk than it is maximizing returns. Rebalancing helps you remove emotions regarding when to buy and when to sell by having some type of trigger for rebalancing so that you're not having to decide in the heat of the moment.

While certain asset classes or sectors may outperform in the short term, they will usually revert to their long-term average. Jack Bogle, the founder of Vanguard, once referred to this as a kind of law of gravity in the stock market, through which returns mysteriously seem to be drawn to the norms of one kind over time. A recent example to illustrate the concept of rebalancing would be to look back to March of 2020. There was so much uncertainty about COVID and the government was issuing a stay-at-home order and forcing businesses to close their doors. So for example, let's say in March, you were invested in 60% stock and 40% bonds. However, March was the time you had predetermined to be your rebalance. You're getting ready to rebalance at a time when the market's lost, in some cases, 10% in a day. The overall market loss was about 33% loss in 33 days during that time.

By March 23 stocks began to recover. If you had stuck with your rebalancing strategy during that time, then you would have sold some of the bonds to buy stocks. You're selling bonds at a time when they're providing safety for your investment portfolio. They're providing the ballast. If you're rebalancing at this time and maintained the discipline to rebalance, and then the stocks started to recover by March 23, 2020, then you were glad that you did sell some of the bonds to purchase more stocks.

The stocks increased substantially from March 23 until the end of the year. Rebalancing can seem counterintuitive, but it is smart. It works by doing the opposite of what we most likely want to do. Warren Buffet is quoted as saying, "Be fearful when others are greedy, be greedy when others are fearful." This is what rebalancing forces you to do, it forces you to sell high and buy low.

WHEN SHOULD YOU REBALANCE?

There are a few different ways to look at rebalancing based on time. Some people will rebalance on a calendar year basis as previously mentioned and the timeframe was based on historical returns of the market. However, this has not held up very well in recent years. Alternatively, some people rebalance monthly. Other people look at rebalancing quarterly or semi-annually or annually. There are many different times that you could look at rebalancing.

The second way that you could look at rebalancing is by a threshold, meaning that you look at the asset allocation and determine if there has been a drift of say 2% or 3% or 5% or 10%. You set up these drift parameters and you say, "Well, I'm only going to rebalance when the portfolio exceeds those drift parameters."

The third option would be to incorporate both time and threshold. For example, you would say, "Okay, I'm going to look at the portfolio every month, but just because I'm looking at it, I'm not necessarily going to rebalance it." If there has been a drift beyond the threshold, again, 2%, 3%, 5%, whatever you're comfortable with, then the higher you let the drift threshold go, the more volatility you would expect in the portfolio.

The more frequently you rebalance, the expectation would be that you're reducing volatility, and reducing standard deviation. If there was anything in investing that always held up to be true, everybody would do it. However, rebalancing doesn't work all the time in the same way.

Research by Vanguard is inconclusive as to the best rebalancing strategy.[26] Vanguard research has determined that none of the major rebalancing approaches holds a distinct and enduring advantage over the others. Vanguard says, "Therefore, the most important consideration is for advisors to apply rebalancing to

---

26 "Financial Planning Perspectives—Getting back on track: A guide to smart rebalancing." Vanguard Group, https://corporate.vanguard.com/content/dam/corp/research/pdf/isggbot_a-042019.pdf. Accessed 4 August 2022.

client portfolios in a consistent and disciplined manner to give clients the best chance for reaching their long-term financial goals."

A few other things to consider would be tax-loss harvesting, cash flow sourcing (especially in retirement), and pulling money out of some accounts as a way to rebalance a portfolio. You will also want to consider the impact of trading costs, which are almost nonexistent for most people these days.

The bottom line is that rebalancing forces you to buy low and sell high. It challenges you to be counterintuitive. Rebalancing is hard because you're selling the good stuff to buy the stuff that doesn't look so good at the time. Rebalancing helps you to remove the emotion from a buy low sell high strategy. There's no one optimal rebalancing schedule, the key to rebalancing is discipline. Rebalancing is more about risk mitigation than it is about optimizing returns, and the people who need to be more concerned with risk mitigation are those preparing to depend on a lifetime of savings and investments to supplement their spending in retirement.

ADDITIONAL RESOURCES

- **Vanguard – Getting Back On Track:** A Guide To Smart Rebalancing https://corporate.vanguard.com/content/dam/corp/research/pdf/isggbot_a-042019.pdf

- **Morningstar – 5 Ways Rebalancing Can Benefit Your Retirement Plan:** https://www.morningstar.com/articles/988423/5-ways-rebalancing-can-benefit-your-retirement-plan

- **Morningstar – Is It Time To Rebalance?:** https://www.morningstar.com/articles/988100/is-it-time-to-rebalance

- **William Bernstein – The Rebalancing Bonus:** http://www.efficientfrontier.com/ef/996/rebal.htm

- **Retirement Researcher – Rebalancing Frequency:** https://retirementresearcher.com/rebalancing-frequency/

- **Michael Kitces – Finding The Optimal Rebalancing Frequency – Time Horizon vs Tolerance Bands:** https://www.kitces.com/blog/best-opportunistic-rebalancing-frequency-time-horizons-vs-tolerance-band-thresholds/

- **Michael Kitces – How Rebalancing Usually Reduces Long-Term Returns (But Is Good Risk Management Anyway):** https://www.kitces.com/blog/how-rebalancing-usually-reduces-long-term-returns-but-is-good-risk-management-anyway/

- **WiserAdvisor – Determining The Optimal Rebalance Frequency:** https://www.wiseradvisor.com/article/determining-the-optimal-rebalancing-frequency-221/

- **AAII – A Question of (RE) balance:** https://www.aaii.com/journal/article/10629-a-question-of-rebalance

- **Statista - The Average Lifespan of a company on the Standard and Poor's 500 Index:** https://www.statista.com/statistics/1259275/average-company-lifespan/#:~:text=In%202020%2C%20the%20average%20lifespan,even%20further%20throughout%20the%202020s.

Chapter 11

MEDICARE

OPTIMIZING MEDICARE SPENDING IN RETIREMENT: 6 TIPS FOR PEOPLE AGE 63 AND UP

Healthcare costs are a non-negotiable line item in every retiree's budget. You can always cancel a vacation or sell an RV, but your medications and trips to the doctor are necessities. While you can't reduce healthcare costs to $0, you can optimize your spending by understanding Medicare and the cost structure. Below you'll find six tips to help you optimize your healthcare spending in retirement.

1. Look For Help With Medicare's Alphabet Soup

Medicare is a complex system with many moving parts and figuring out the right plan for you can be tricky. Evidence shows that just 1 in 20 people choose the drug plan that minimizes their out-of-pocket expenses. Figuring out how the system works can be a full-time job. Thankfully, many people volunteer their time to help retirees figure this system out. You can find local resources by entering your zip code at **ElderCare.acl.gov.**

As you prepare to meet with someone locally, it can help to know:

- **Medicare Part A** covers hospitalizations, skilled nursing facilities, hospice, lab tests, surgery, and home healthcare. Anyone who paid into Medicare for at least 30 quarters will receive Medicare Part A without paying a premium.

- **Medicare Part B** is most similar to health insurance from an employer-sponsored health insurance plan. It covers doctor's visits, outpatient care, home healthcare, durable medical equipment, and some preventive services. The standard rate for Medicare Part B is $170.10 per month as of 2022.

- **Medicare Part D**[27] covers prescription drug costs. The average monthly cost is $42 per month, but premiums vary based on coverage.

- **Medigap** isn't part of Medicare. Instead, these supplemental plans cover services that aren't covered by Medicare Parts A, B and D. These are standardized plans (with letters A-N in most states) that offer a variety of coverage options. You can learn more about the plan offerings on **Medicare.gov**. Medigap plans can help you save money overall, but you need to be careful to find the right plan to fit your needs and the best deal on the right

---

27 "Medicare Part D: A First Look at Prescription Drug Plans in 2020 - Issue Brief." KFF, 14 November 2019, https://www.kff.org/report-section/medicare-part-d-a-first-look-at-prescription-drug-plans-in-2020-issue-brief/.

plan. Research from ValuePenguin[28] showed that premiums for Plan A ranged from $147 to $784 per month.

- **Medicare Part C** (also known as Medicare Advantage)[29] are plans that Bundle Medicare Parts A, B, and D into a single plan. Enrollees can opt for a Medicare Advantage Plan rather than paying for each part individually.

2. Enroll On Time

People who are 65 years old must enroll in Medicare Part A and B unless they have a qualified exception. Anyone who fails to enroll faces steep penalties for the remainder of their time in Medicare. Those who do not sign up for Medicare on time will pay a 10% penalty for each 12-month period that they were not enrolled in Medicare Part B. They will pay a 12% Penalty for each 12-month period they were not enrolled in Medicare Part D[30].

Those penalties can stack up over time. A person who enrolls 3 years late for Medicare Part B will pay a 30% penalty for life. In 2021, a 3-year late enrollee will pay $221.13 per month instead of the standard $171.10. The average Prescription Drug Plan (Part

28 Guinan, Stephanie. "4 Best Medicare Supplement Plans for 2022." ValuePenguin, 2 August 2022, https://www.valuepenguin.com/best-medicare-supplement-plans.

29 "Home Medicare Advantage Plans How do Medicare Advantage Plans work?" Medicare, https://www.medicare.gov/types-of-medicare-health-plans/medicare-advantage-plans/how-do-medicare-advantage-plans-work.

30 "Home Your Medicare costs Part B costs Part B late enrollment penalty." Medicare, https://www.medicare.gov/your-medicare-costs/part-b-costs/part-b-late-enrollment-penalty.

D) cost was $42 per month in 2020. A person who enrolls three years too late will pay $57.12 per month.

Medicare.gov gives detailed information about when each person must enroll in Medicare, so check out the site around age 63-64 to determine whether you should enroll.

If you already receive Social Security Benefits, enrollment is automatic. The Social Security Administration handles enrollment for them. Everyone else needs to think about enrollment, even those who are still working.

If you aren't covered by an employer plan, enroll at age 65. Even if you aren't taking Social Security checks, you need to enroll in Medicare Part A and B at age 65. You can start enrolling 3 months before you turn 65.

If you are working, don't assume you have an exemption. People who are covered by an employer-sponsored health insurance plan may be allowed to defer Medicare enrollment, but that isn't always the case. People who work for a company with fewer than 20 employees, who are part of the health plan, must enroll in Medicare at age 65. Those who work for larger companies should check with Human Resources to ensure that their health plan qualifies them for exemption. Once you stop working, you need to enroll within 8 months of your coverage ceasing.

3. Know The Deadlines

People on Medicare always have options to change plans once per year between October 15 and December 7. If your health status has changed, or prices have gone up, it is a good idea to research a better plan during this window. Those who are enrolled in Medicare Advantage Plans can change plans between January 1 and the end of March. People who want to switch between "Standard" Medicare and Medicare "Advantage" Plans should not stop enrollment in one plan until they have confirmed that new coverage has started with the other plan.

4. Consider Total Cost

People trying to save money on healthcare costs may often choose the plans with the lowest premiums. This is a good way to cut costs, but it can backfire. People who have regular doctors visits or who require medication may see their out-of-pocket costs overshadow premium costs. When you're considering which plan, consider the whole cost, not just the upfront premium costs. The Medicare website makes it easy to compare real costs between various plans.

5. Seek Financial Assistance

If you're struggling to pay for prescription drug costs, you may qualify for Medicare Extra Help. This benefit can be worth up to $5,000 per year. If you have limited assets, and you have a lower income, this assistance can help you obtain needed medications at a reasonable price. Be sure to keep this resource in mind if your retirement budget is slim.

6. Ask For Reconsideration

If you're someone who has a high income before retirement, then you may be faced with unexpectedly high Medicare costs. Those with incomes above $88,000 ($176,000 for filing jointly) will pay higher premiums for Medicare Part B. The income that Medicare considers is your Social Security Income from 2 years previous. Because of this, people who retire after a few years of high earning may see higher premiums unless they request reconsideration.

However, Medicare allows enrollees to request reconsideration based on a change in circumstances. Qualifying changes include stopping work, divorce, death, marriage, or a loss of income.

If you earned $95,000 in your last year of work, but expect to have a retirement income of $42,000, you may qualify for a reduction in premiums. To do this you must request an IRMAA (Income Related Monthly Adjustment Amount) which can be done through the Social Security Administration.

HEALTHCARE IN RETIREMENT TAKEAWAYS

Planning for healthcare costs in retirement is intimidating. With out-of-pocket costs rising quickly, many people worry that a limited nest egg won't be able to cover all their costs. But by understanding the Medicare system, and regularly evaluating your needs, you can find the coverage that optimizes costs and coverage during your retirement years.

ADDITIONAL RESOURCES:

- **Taking the Mystery out of Medicare with Dr. Katy Votava.** Sound Retirement Planning. http://soundretirementplanning.com/231-taking-the-mystery-out-of-medicare-with-dr-katy-votava

Chapter 12

HIRING A FINANCIAL ADVISOR

The Retirement Budget Calculator was developed for the "Do-it-yourself money nerd." However, according to the data we'll discuss in more detail below, those who utilize an advisor do considerably better than those who don't. We want to foster financial literacy and the greatest possible outcomes for people. For the majority of people, this implies they should engage the services of a financial advisor. This chapter is designed to help you understand why working with an advisor can be beneficial and what to look for when choosing one.

One of the mistakes many people make when working on their retirement planning is they ask for the advice of a family member, a friend, a coworker, or even a general financial advice giver. While these individuals may genuinely want to help, chances are that they don't know all of the specifics about your situation to provide you with expert advice. All they are equipped to do is to tell you what worked for them and to offer their opinion.

Retirement involves many different areas of expertise. You must consider how to maximize your Social Security, pensions, and other income sources, as well as create tax-efficient income. A financial advisor should be trained in how to preserve a lifetime of hard work and make a plan so that you don't run out of money during your lifetime. A skilled practitioner will be looking at your investments, insurance, estate plan, entitlements, pensions, inflation, and taxes to make sure that every area of your financial life is coordinated and optimized so you will feel confident in your ability to meet your goals. The decisions you make as you transition into and through retirement will be some of the most important that you may ever make.

Remember, you may spend as many years retired as you did working. Twenty-five years of unemployment is a long time, and you won't be adding to your investments anymore. What you have is what you have, and you need to make sure it's going to last as long as you do. The last thing you want to have to worry about is going back to work after ten years of retirement because you made a financial mistake. It's not fair to your friends and family members to place the burden of your questions on their shoulders. Instead, make sure you find an expert who specializes in retirement planning.

AVOID HIGH FEES AND COMMISSIONS

You need to understand the impact fees can have on your investment portfolio. By diversifying your investments, you are diversifying your investments for principal preservation and growth. However, you are also moving your investments to fee-efficient accounts. If you had all your investments in no-load mutual funds and the average fee on those funds was 0.5% per year on $1,000,000, your annual expense would be $5,000. If you are paying an advisor an additional 1% per year, then you are looking at a total annual expense of $15,000. An advisor's fee will be disclosed and should be easy to understand. If you currently own funds, it can be hard to uncover all of the fees that you're paying. Of course, your prospectus will list fees, but a quick way to help uncover all of the fees you're paying is to use a tool at PersonalFund.com. It compares exchange-traded funds versus mutual funds and helps to uncover all fees.

I'm a fan of low-cost investing using asset allocation as the foundation for maximizing risk-adjusted returns. Bogle is one of my heroes in our industry and an advocate for smaller investors. Vanguard built its firm around low-cost index mutual funds and currently is one of the leaders in exchange-traded funds (ETFs). Both vehicles have advantages and disadvantages.

One common complaint about ETFs is the brokerage fees associated with buying and selling these investments. If you intend to do a lot of buying and selling within the portfolio of ETFs, then you should use a more fee-efficient tool to track an index like the ETFs close cousin, the Index Mutual Fund, instead. Today, many firms offer no-cost trades on things like ETFs. They are more liquid and can be very tax efficient, which is important for your non-qualified accounts.

Either choice serves the same basic purpose. Both are excellent vehicles for helping you achieve your long-term growth goals. ETFs and Index Mutual Funds are both very efficient tools for creating global broad-based diversified portfolios among asset classes and sectors, and they should be considered as part of your overall diversification strategy.

IS IT WORTH IT TO PAY AN ADVISOR?

This is a question of value versus cost, with a price paid for something and then a benefit gained. Some things to consider, while you think about this question in terms of paying fees to hire an advisor, are ...

- Should you be looking for the cheapest financial advisor?

- Is finding the cheapest advisor important to you?

- Would that be on your list of requirements or qualities you're seeking when hiring an advisor?

One of the distinctions I think is crucial to make is the difference between investing fees versus the cost of hiring a financial advisor who takes a whole-picture view of your finances. Bogle is quoted as saying, "The case for indexing isn't based on the Efficient-Market Hypothesis. It's based on simple arithmetic of the Cost Matter Hypothesis. In many areas of the market, there will be a loser for every winner. So, on average, investors will get the return of the market less fees."

Bogle preached for years that costs matter. He said they matter more than past performance. Remember the Vanguard Group as well as the Vanguard Mutual Funds and ETFs have been a driving force in helping drive down investment fees, which has been a good thing for the individual investor. We'll look at some of the other studies released by Vanguard on advisor fees.

IS IT POSSIBLE THAT SOME PEOPLE DON'T REQUIRE AN ADVISOR?

I've met a few individuals that are fantastic at both financial planning and investment management. They are part of that 10-20 percentile of people who can consider doing financial planning and investment management on their own. I recognize that this is a small subset. These people are similar to those mechanics who like to work on their own car, the mechanic that says, "I don't want to hire a mechanic. I don't want to pay the mechanic's costs. I'd rather go down to the parts store and buy the part myself than hire a mechanic." They're good at it, they have the tools and expertise. For some people, I believe it's a viable option to have them create a plan and manage the investments.

But for the majority of Americans, if you consider the studies that have been done, I think you will agree that it is worth it to pay an advisor a fee. If we look at what the value is that an advisor can bring to you, it's more than just investment management, it's comprehensive financial planning. This means having someone who looks at all aspects of your financial life.

RESEARCH SUGGESTS THAT ADVISED INVESTORS BUILD MORE WEALTH?

There was a survey that was completed in Canada[31] and the research indicates that advised investors build more wealth when

---

31   Bourque, Paul. "Canadian investors value advice." Investment Executive, 18 September 2019, https://www.investmentexecutive.com/inside-track_/paul-bourque/canadian-investors-value-advice/.

compared to non-advised investors. The study controlled for nearly 50 socioeconomic and attitudinal differences and what they found was that after 15 years, people that had advisors versus those that did not have advisors had 3.9 times more assets. An advised individual's net worth had improved significantly compared to those who did not have an advisor.

SHOULD YOU CONSIDER PAYING FOR AN ADVISOR?

The Vanguard Group developed the Vanguard Advisor's Alpha[32], which explores the value of working with a financial advisor. It may seem counterintuitive or illogical that the company responsible for driving down investing costs would also be the company responsible for recommending people pay fees to financial advisors. This begs the question, can we trust Vanguard and their research? Are they a trustworthy company? Are they attempting to persuade individuals to use financial advisors? Do they have a hidden agenda? Do they have any ulterior motives?

There are two sides to this equation. Advisors need to be able to create value, preserve value, and perpetuate it. If advisors are not doing those, why would an individual continue working with them and paying their fees? That wouldn't make any sense. Individuals are responsible for understanding what they are paying in fees,

---

32 "The buck stops here: Vanguard money market funds Vanguard research September 2016 Putting a value on your value: Quantifying Vanguard Advisor's Alpha." Vanguard Advisors, https://www.investmentofficer.nl/sites/default/files/ISGQVAA.pdf. Accessed 4 August 2022.

"Is It Worth the Money to Hire a Financial Advisor?" The Balance, https://www.thebalance.com/should-you-hire-a-financial-advisor-4120717.

as well as for understanding what to expect for those fees. So, as we look at this Vanguard research, the Advisor's Alpha, here's what they've concluded in their white paper. It says, "Putting a value on your value is as subjective and unique as each individual investor." For some, the value of working with an advisor is peace of mind. For others, working with an advisor can add about 3% in net returns. If the advisor charges 1%, then they're implying that they'll provide returns greater than 3% net.

Over time, individuals will earn 3% net per year on average. These returns won't always come directly each year, but over time.

Advisors add value in the following ways:

- **Cost-effective implementation and lowering expense ratios.** The study allots 34 basis points for the efficient deployment of investment vehicles by Advisors. The Vanguard Group believes that advisors add value by assisting clients in lowering their overall fee structure.

- **Portfolio rebalancing.** The study allots about 26 basis points for having an advisor, which is attributed to portfolio rebalancing. Rebalancing forces you to buy low and sell high and the process of rebalancing can be counterintuitive. According to Vanguard, that's worth roughly 26 basis points. Vanguard assigns 1.5% to advisors on this topic of behavioral coaching. Most individuals, they argue, get investing wrong in that they buy high and sell low. According to the Dalbar Studies[33] investors' gains are significantly lower than even those of the mutual funds they're invested in. Many individuals make the error of purchasing at the wrong time, then selling when things start to go bad. In situations of tremendous worry or exuberance, an advisor's work begins to come into play. There's something to be said for having someone else looking over your shoulder and offering you advice and assistance throughout the moments and events when it matters most.

- **Asset Allocation.** The next area that the Vanguard Group says contributes approximately a 0.75% value is asset location. The primary goal of asset location is tax efficiency to make sure you have the appropriate type of assets in the correct buckets. IRAs, non-qualified, Roth IRAs and brokerage accounts are all popular among individuals. A financial advisor makes sure that the right investments are in the right accounts.

- **Spending Strategies and Withdrawal Order.** Having spending strategies and having a withdrawal order were the last two elements that provided significant value, according to Vanguards' white paper. Vanguard says that the value can add up to 1.1% to investors.

---

33 Coleman, Murray. "Dalbar QAIB 2022: Investors are Still Their Own Worst Enemies." Index Fund Advisors, Inc., 4 April 2022, https://www.ifa.com/articles/dalbar_2016_qaib_investors_still_their_worst_enemy/. Accessed 4 August 2022.

We're talking about paying a 1% fee for a 3% return. Is it worth it? On a one million dollar advised investment account, a 1% fee is $10,000 and a 3% return is $30,000. Is that something you'd be willing to do?

WHAT DOES THE MORNINGSTAR STUDY SAY ABOUT THE VALUE OF FINANCIAL ADVISORS?

Morningstar, a respected firm that most people are familiar with, began as a fund research business but has expanded into several areas over the years. They wrote a paper called *Alpha, Beta, and Now Gamma*[34]. In it they said, "We focus on five important financial planning decisions and techniques."

- The first one is a total wealth framework to determine the optimal asset allocation.

- The second is a dynamic withdrawal strategy.

---

34 "Alpha, Beta, and Now…Gamma." Morningstar, Inc., 28 August 2013, https://www.morningstar.com/content/dam/marketing/shared/research/foundational/677796-AlphaBetaGamma.pdf.

"The Gamma Factor and the Value of Financial Advice - Claude Montmarquette, Nathalie Viennot-Briot." CIRANO, https://www.cirano.qc.ca/files/publications/2016s-35.pdf.

Investment Planning Counsel, https://www.investmentplanningcounsel.ca/web/guest//archive/article/757576.

"The Cost Matters Hypothesis." Morningstar, https://www.morningstar.com/articles/740544/the-cost-matters-hypothesis.

- Third comes incorporating guaranteed income products, such as annuities.

- The fourth is tax-efficient allocation decisions.

- Lastly, a portfolio optimization that includes a proxy for the investors in implicit or explicit liabilities.

Furthermore, they go on to say that each of these five gamma components create value for retirees. Given the paper's assumptions about risk aversion and other variables, when combined they can be expected to generate about 22.6% more certainty equivalent income when compared to a simplistic, static withdrawal strategy, according to our analysis. The "certainty equivalent" represents the amount of guaranteed money an investor would accept now instead of taking a risk of getting more money at a future date. The way that they frame this is interesting to me.

This additional certainty equivalent income has the same impact on expected utility as an arithmetic alpha of 1.59% and thereby represents a significant potential increase in portfolio efficiency for retirement income for retirees.

Expected utility theory is used as a tool for analyzing situations in which individuals must make a decision without knowing the outcomes that may result from that decision, and arithmetic alpha is what helps investors determine how much a portfolio's realized return differs from the return it should have achieved.

WHAT DOES ENVESTNET PORTFOLIO MANAGEMENT CONSULTANTS CONCLUDE ABOUT ADVISORS?

Another study was done by an organization called Envestnet Portfolio Management Consultants[35]. They also looked to see the value of financial advice for individuals. They observed the following areas:

- financial planning,

- asset class selection and allocation,

- investment selection,

- rebalancing, and

- tax management.

Each element can contribute alpha or excess return over a given benchmark. They conclude that "according to our research, the combination of successfully implementing these sources has produced around 3% of value added annually." They explain each one and assign a figure to quantify the value that it generates. The first one was asset location, and they say that that's worth 50 basis points or about half a percent.

They go on to say, "Our research has determined that employing a strategy of selecting active mutual fund managers, according to certain risk-adjusted return characteristics, can add 67 basis points of value annually to a diversified portfolio. Implementing

---

35 "Capital Sigma: The Advisor Advantage | Envestnet PMC." Envestnet PMC |, https://www.investpmc.com/insights/white-papers/capital-sigma-advisor-advantage.

the portfolio with passive investments can add 61 basis points of value each year."

In addressing the fourth pillar, the advisor added value and systematic portfolio rebalancing. They said, "We demonstrate the advantages of regular systematic rebalancing and how it can help to control risk by reducing portfolio volatility and enhancing returns. We contrast the effects of more or less frequent rebalancing and offer a rationale to explain why an annual rebalancing frequency is optimal. The process of systematically rebalancing a diversified portfolio can add 30 basis points of value each year compared with a naive strategy of rebalancing once every three years."

The Envestnet study also said tax management can add about 100 basis points or 1% per year.

So, again, these are areas where financial advisors are shown to be beneficial for their clients:

- 50 basis points or half a percent for financial planning

- 52 basis points asset class selection and allocation

- 67 basis points for investment selection, active management (or 61 basis points for passive management)

- 30 basis points for systematic rebalancing

- 100 basis points for tax management

That totals 299 basis points or approximately 3% per year in value that a financial advisor can add. The point of all of this is that you have to compare costs to the value received.

CAN YOU TRUST THESE STUDIES?

Well there is one question you have to answer. Are these studies true or false?

If these studies are true, then why wouldn't you want to benefit from paying a fee to work with an advisor since the studies show conclusively that by hiring a good financial advisor you'd actually have the potential to increase your overall earnings than doing it on your own?

If these studies are false, then in order to believe that they're false, you have to believe that all of these different studies are being done so that advisors can justify the fees that they charge and that the people who have done these studies are lying or exaggerating the numbers because they have a vested interest in the outcome. In believing so, you also have to believe that a company like Vanguard, that was responsible for driving the fees down, is also the company now that's trying to get you to pay fees. Why would they do this? Because if you make more money, then they make more money and their studies show that you will actually make more money by hiring and paying a fee to an advisor than by them just lowering their investment fees.

Or maybe you didn't know that these studies existed, in which case you were just flying blind. However now that you know these studies exist you have a decision to make. Should I hire an advisor and get more bang for my buck in the long run or just go it alone to save on fees, but lose out on the potential growth an advised portfolio could bring?

In the end, the result we want is for you to have a good retirement.

- We want you to have cash flow.

- We want you to pay your fair share in taxes, but not a penny more.

- We want you to only pay fees that produce valuable outcomes.

- We want you to have an investment strategy that's right for you, one that's right for the amount of risk that you're going to be comfortable with.

- We want to make sure that you have a good healthcare plan. What if somebody gets sick?

- We want to know that the plan is going to continue. If the person who used to run the numbers is no longer available to do it, or they simply don't have the capacity to do so, we want to make sure that you're not leaving a big mess for future generations or a surviving spouse.

There's a lot that goes into putting together a successful retirement financial strategy, and there is a lot of responsibility. Is it worth it to hire an advisor? For most of you, the answer will be yes.

10 QUESTIONS TO ASK BEFORE HIRING A FINANCIAL ADVISOR

A lot of people want help managing their financial life, but hiring a financial advisor can be intimidating. What should you look for in a financial advisor? How can you be sure that your financial advisor will be worth the cost?

Oftentimes, finding the right financial advisor involves interviewing a few advisors, and finding the one that "clicks" with you. But you don't want to meet a potential advisor unprepared. So, before you interview a financial advisor, here are ten questions you can ask. These questions won't just help you weed out a bad egg, they'll help you clarify what you want from a financial advisor.

1. Do You Have Experience Helping People Like Me?

Most financial advisors specialize in helping certain types of people. For example, some advisors help people as they approach retirement age. These advisors typically have in-depth knowledge about Social Security, retirement budget planning, and retirement withdrawal strategies. Other financial advisors specialize in helping business owners create investment strategies after selling businesses.

Still, others work with clients in their 30s and 40s who are working to develop a nest egg. An advisor who works with people like you will generally be better suited to helping you achieve your personal goals. It might also mean that you change financial advisers as you transition from working to retirement to get the expertise you need for the slice of life you're in.

2. How Do You Provide Value To People Like Me?

Certain financial advisors focus on providing value through their asset management practice. Some focus on tax planning. Others help you create and maintain financial plans in an ever-changing economy. Some financial advisors focus on risk mitigation through insurance and income planning. The value an advisor provides should line up with your reason for hiring that advisor. If your goal is to plan for retirement, but the advisor helps with business tax planning, then the relationship won't be a great fit.

3. What Are Your Credentials?

Many people who operate as financial advisors have some sort of credentialing and the type of advice an advisor gives is likely to be heavily influenced by their credentials.

These are a few of the most common credentials, and what they mean for you.

Typical Designations For Financial Advisors

Financial advisors can often list pages of letters after their name, but not all designations are created equally. If you're looking for a long-term relationship with a financial advisor, these are the certifications you should seek:

- **Certified Financial Planner (CFP)**. CFPs specialize in creating financial plans that help you to achieve your short and long-term goals. All CFPs must work in the best interest of their clients, have at least 2 years of experience and have passed an exam. In addition to managing your investment portfolio, CFPs may make recommendations to buy certain types of insurance, to reduce your debt, or to reduce your tax burden.

- **Chartered Financial Consultant (ChFC).** Similar to CFPs, ChFCs focus on the essentials of financial planning (such as investing, saving, and risk management). ChFCs must prove competence in fundamental financial planning, but do not have to pass a board exam.

- **Retirement Income Certified Professional (RICP).** This designation equips advisors with the knowledge to effectively manage the transition from asset accumulation during a client's working years to asset decumulation in retirement. RICP enables the advisor to demonstrate tremendous value by delivering smart strategies for creating secure, sustainable income for a client's retirement. All RICPs must have 3 years of experience, have passed an exam and must obtain 15 hours of continuing education every two years.

- **Chartered Financial Analyst (CFA).** CFAs specialize in portfolio management techniques and investment analysis. They must pass three exams and have at least four years of professional experience to achieve this designation. By completing and passing all three exams, CFAs also show competency in wealth planning techniques.

Other Financial Advisor Designations

In addition to the typical financial advisor designations, these are a few designations that they might also have. It's important to note that these designations demonstrate proficiency in at least one area of financial planning. However, advisors with these designations may not be able to help you with comprehensive planning.

- **Certified public accountant (CPA).** A CPA can provide tax advice (including tax planning advice) to you. They don't just prepare your tax documents each April. Rather, CPAs can give advice about how to structure your business and your finances to minimize your tax burden. Even if your primary financial advisor isn't a CPA, you'll probably have some interactions with CPAs as you develop your financial roadmap.

- **Chartered Life Underwriter (CLU).** A chartered life underwriter is someone who is licensed to sell life insurance products. These could include everything from simple term life insurance policies to complex annuities with life insurance riders. Most people will need to buy life insurance at some point during their financial journey, so you'll want advice from a CLU. However, a CLU that doesn't have other credentials may not be the best long-term advisor for you.

- **Juris Doctor (JD).** A JD indicates that a person has a law degree. If they've passed the Bar Exam in your state, they can also practice law. Estate planning lawyers, some small business financial advisors, bankruptcy lawyers, and other debt-relief lawyers will have a JD. When you need someone to help you through the legal parts of a financial issue, you'll want to enlist the help of someone with a JD and experience giving financial advice.

- **Series 3, 6, 7, 24, 51, 63, 65 and 66 licenses.** The Financial Industry Regulatory Authority (FINRA) and the North American Securities Administrators Association (NASAA) issue licenses for professionals that want to buy and sell stocks, bonds, and other commodities. Almost anyone that wants to provide investment advice must have this licensing, so any financial advisor should have one or more of these licenses. However, most financial advisors will also have other designations to show their competence as an advisor.

4. Are you a fiduciary?

A fiduciary financial advisor is someone who is legally obligated to work in your best interest. If a financial advisor isn't a fiduciary, they only need to meet a suitability standard. A suitability standard means that the advisor will only make recommendations that are suitable for you, even if the advisor knows of better alternatives. If you intend to have an ongoing relationship with a financial advisor, you generally want that advisor to meet a fiduciary standard.

5. How do you get paid?

Generally, when we hire someone, we know exactly how they get paid. We pay the plumber $150 to fix a leaky pipe. You'll pay a tutor $25 per hour to teach you Spanish. But in the financial advice industry, payments aren't always clear. Financial advisors can get paid through fees (including a portfolio management fee or an hourly fee), or through commissions (earning money based on the products they sell). Some advisors are paid using both methods. If that's the case, it's helpful to clarify which products they earn commissions on (often on insurance products), and which products they do not earn commissions for selling.

6. Do you ever get paid to recommend certain products over others?

Certain investment advisors, especially those with just broker designations, might recommend products based on the commission that they earn. While earning a commission on a product has been an acceptable way for financial advisors to earn money, it's important for customers to understand that the commission may be part of the reason an advisor is recommending a product to you. If you know a financial advisor earns a commission by selling certain products or investments, you should make sure you understand how these recommendations work and why they are valuable in your overall retirement financial plan.

7. Do you have any complaints against you? What were the results?

Properly licensed financial advisors have a profile that includes complaints against the advisor. You can check on their profile through FINRA's Broker Check at *BrokerCheck.finra.org* or the SEC's Investment Advisor Public Disclosure at *AdviserInfo.sec.gov.* A complaint against an advisor may be a red flag, but it shouldn't necessarily disqualify an advisor from your consideration. Some of the complaints that make the record could have been completely unfounded, and the advisor can easily explain the situation.

8. How often can we expect to meet if I hire you?

Sometimes financial advisors will meet with you just a few times. For example, estate planning lawyers may only meet with you twice, once to create an estate plan, and again to review it. After that, your only meetings will be to update it. Other financial advisors will meet as often as once per month or once per quarter. These advisors typically want to stay in the loop and help you as you make big spending decisions such as buying a house or a car. Some will offer only an annual review, but will allow you to schedule other appointments as needed.

9. Where can I see my information?

If you're hiring someone who will manage your assets, you should be able to easily access your personal information (such as account balances and your investment allocation).

In particular, you should know the status of your investment portfolio, and the beneficiaries on your accounts or insurance policies. Many advisors offer information through a website or online portal, but some may send monthly or quarterly statements instead. If you're investing in proprietary investments such as Master Limited Partnerships, Non-Traded Real Estate Investment Trusts, or other similar investments, you should expect to get regular quarterly financial updates from the investment company. If your advisor cannot clearly explain how you'll get access to your investment information, this should be a huge red flag for you. The so-called advisor may actually be selling you a fraudulent product.

10. Do you work with a team?

No financial advisor can be an expert in every aspect of financial planning, but that doesn't mean a financial advisor will leave you without a solution. Some advisors will help you by referring you to specialists to give you help in areas such as estate planning or tax preparation. Others will have an in-house team to cover these needs. It can be important to clarify what a financial advisor refers to as an out-of-house team, since you may pay additional fees for those services as well.

Chapter 13

FINAL THOUGHTS

"The best way to predict the future is to create it." – Peter Drucker

Imagine having a financial summary prepared for you by your digital financial advisor at the crack of dawn. This advisor is working on your behalf, securely, consistently and 24 hours a day. Your digital advisor informs you that your retirement is on track and that you can spend $321 today if you want. It has transferred the cash from your investment account to your checking account for your enjoyment, because this was your preference. Your virtual financial advisor assists you in paying less tax and ensuring that adjustments are made regularly to optimize your financial future. Your retirement plan, budget, investments, insurance, and taxes will all be optimized for you. You don't have to worry about the stress, the hassle, or the complexity of managing it all. Your virtual advisor does it for you.

Machine learning and artificial intelligence will tackle the difficult financial questions and after running thousands of scenarios, help you select your preferred outcomes. It will serve you first and learn from you, securely and subtly, only making decisions that you have approved in advance.

This particular future is not here yet, but this is the future we are working towards.

The Retirement Budget Calculator currently looks and feels like a comfortable spreadsheet, with easy to read charts and graphs. But our longer vision for the future is to simplify the outlook of your financial future so there is no more guesswork. We are working to make the technology serve you, without making you learn more confusing things like tax law, in the days of your retirement. Who has time for that?

For most of my career as a Registered Investment Adviser Representative, I've worked with people to help them in the areas of retirement planning, insurance, and investment management. I have found that individuals frequently make emotional decisions that can result in costly errors.

Many people are hesitant to live their best lives because they're afraid they'll run out of money in retirement. Instead of living in bright optimism, they stay locked up afraid to make a mistake.

The truth is that almost all of us need the help of seasoned financial professionals. Many individuals today live isolated, either in rural areas or in walls of their own making, afraid to talk about money, and do not have access to a friendly local financial advisor. Or simply do not have enough money to meet the investment minimums that many advisors require to become a new client. Why should it be so hard to get financial help to have a great retirement?

In the USA, there are currently 10,000 people turning 65 every day. Many of whom want to retire, but they have questions and don't really know where they stand. Additionally, 40% of financial advisors are themselves expected to retire in the next 10 years. Put those two stats together and it shows that as a society, we simply don't have enough financial professionals to serve everyone who needs financial coaching or investment help. Technology will need to step in to support the future of America's retirees. This is a fact.

The Retirement Budget Calculator is helping to democratize retirement. We are giving people a greater sense of clarity, confidence and helping them experience more freedom by having a retirement financial plan. This is a plan where they are in charge. The technology serves them and gives them peace of mind.

Today, the calculator has you simply input your data, and help you answer a few questions to best analyze your financial information and goals.

The following three questions can be used to map your retirement planning:

- How long will you live?

- How much do you spend?

- How much have you saved?

Everything else in retirement is about minor tweaks and optimization. Does it sound simple? We hope so. We have worked hard to give you a blueprint to financial peace of mind in your retirement.

While we don't have artificial intelligence programs ready to serve you yet, we are going to get there. We know that technology is going to be the biggest differentiator to helping you grow your portfolio, plan your expenses, and help you craft the optimal retirement.

Want to learn more? Go to ***RetirementBudgetCalculator.com*** and give it a try. We are building better retirement tools to give you the brightest, most confident future possible.

Join us, we would love to serve you!

WORKS CITED

Investopedia: Sharper insight, better investing., http://investopedia.com.

Retirement Budget Calculator - Do I have enough to retire?, http://retirementbudgetcalculator.com..

Eldercare Locator, http://eldercare.acl.gov..

Welcome to Medicare | Medicare, http://medicare.gov.

Personal Fund: Home, http://personalfund.com.

"Actuarial Life Table." Social Security, https://www.ssa.gov/oact/STATS/table4c6.html.

"Alpha, Beta, and Now…Gamma." Morningstar, Inc., 28 August 2013, https://www.morningstar.com/content/dam/marketing/shared/research/foundational/677796-AlphaBetaGamma.pdf.

"Benefits Planner: Retirement | Delayed Retirement Credits | SSA." Social Security, https://www.ssa.gov/benefits/retirement/planner/delayret.html.

Bengen, William P. "DETERMINING WITHDRAWAL RATES USING HISTORICAL DATA." Retail Investor .org, https://www.retailinvestor.org/pdf/Bengen1.pdf.

Benz, Christine. "5 Ways Rebalancing Can Benefit Your Retirement Plan." Morningstar, 17 June 2020, https://www.morningstar.com/articles/988423/5-ways-rebalancing-can-benefit-your-retirement-plan.

Benz, Christine. "Is It Time to Rebalance?" Morningstar, 12 June 2020, https://www.morningstar.com/articles/988100/is-it-time-to-rebalance.

Benz, Christine. "Should Your Withdrawals Mirror Your RMDs?" Morningstar, 7 March 2019, https://www.morningstar.com/articles/918416/should-your-withdrawals-mirror-your-rmds.

Bernstein, William J. "The Rebalancing Bonus." Efficient Frontier, http://www.efficientfrontier.com/ef/996/rebal.htm. Accessed 4 August 2022.

Bourque, Paul. "Canadian investors value advice." Investment Executive, 18 September 2019, https://www.investmentexecutive.com/inside-track_/paul-bourque/canadian-investors-value-advice/.

"The buck stops here: Vanguard money market funds Vanguard research September 2016 Putting a value on your value: Quantifying Vanguard Advisor's Alpha." Vanguard Advisors, https://www.investmentofficer.nl/sites/default/files/ISGQVAA.pdf.

"Capital Sigma: The Advisor Advantage | Envestnet PMC." Envestnet PMC |, https://www.investpmc.com/insights/white-papers/capital-sigma-advisor-advantage.

Clark, D. "• Average company lifespan 2020." Statista, 27 August 2021, https://www.statista.com/statistics/1259275/average-company-lifespan/.

Coleman, Murray. "Dalbar QAIB 2022: Investors are Still Their Own Worst Enemies." Index Fund Advisors, Inc., 4 April 2022, https://www.ifa.com/articles/dalbar_2016_qaib_investors_still_their_worst_enemy/.

"The Cost Matters Hypothesis." Morningstar, Inc., https://www.morningstar.com/articles/740544/the-cost-matters-hypothesis.

"Determinants of Portfolio Performance: Financial Analysts Journal: Vol 42, No 4." Taylor & Francis Online, 31 December 2018, https://www.tandfonline.com/doi/abs/10.2469/faj.v42.n4.39.

"Determining the Optimal Rebalancing Frequency." WiserAdvisor, https://www.wiseradvisor.com/article/determining-the-optimal-rebalancing-frequency-221/.

Downey, Lucas. "Efficient Market Hypothesis (EMH) Definition." Investopedia, https://www.investopedia.com/terms/e/efficientmarkethypothesis.asp.

"Explaining The Capital Asset Pricing Model (CAPM)." Investopedia, https://www.investopedia.com/articles/06/capm.asp.

"Fama-French Three-Factor Model - Components, Formula & Uses." Corporate Finance Institute, 18 February 2022, https://corporatefinanceinstitute.com/resources/knowledge/finance/fama-french-three-factor-model/.

"The Fed - Table: Survey of Consumer Finances, 1989 - 2019." Board of Governors of the Federal Reserve System, https://www.federalreserve.gov/econres/scf/dataviz/scf/table/#series:Net_Worth;demographic:agecl;population:all;units:mean;range:1989,2019.

"Financial Planning Perspectives—Getting back on track: A guide to smart rebalancing." Vanguard Group, https://corporate.vanguard.com/content/dam/corp/research/pdf/isggbot_a-042019.pdf.

"The Gamma Factor and the Value of Financial Advice - Claude Montmarquette, Nathalie Viennot-Briot." CIRANO, https://www.cirano.qc.ca/files/publications/2016s-35.pdf.

Guinan, Stephanie. "4 Best Medicare Supplement Plans for 2022." ValuePenguin, 2 August 2022, https://www.valuepenguin.com/best-medicare-supplement-plans.

Guyton, Jonathan T., and William J. Klinger. "CFP." Cornerstone Wealth Advisors, https://cornerstonewealthadvisors.com/wp-content/uploads/2014/09/08-06_WebsiteArticle.pdf.

"Home Medicare Advantage Plans How do Medicare Advantage Plans work?" Medicare, https://www.medicare.gov/types-of-medicare-health-plans/medicare-advantage-plans/how-do-medicare-advantage-plans-work.

"Home Your Medicare costs Part B costs Part B late enrollment penalty." Medicare, https://www.medicare.gov/your-medicare-costs/part-b-costs/part-b-late-enrollment-penalty.

"IRA Required Minimum Distribution Worksheet." IRS, https://www.irs.gov/pub/irs-tege/uniform_rmd_wksht.pdf.

"Is It Worth the Money to Hire a Financial Advisor?" The Balance, https://www.thebalance.com/should-you-hire-a-financial-advisor-4120717.

Kitces, Michael. "Optimal Rebalancing – Time Horizons Vs Tolerance Bands." Michael Kitces, 4 May 2016, https://www.kitces.com/blog/best-opportunistic-rebalancing-frequency-time-horizons-vs-tolerance-band-thresholds/.

Kitces, Michael. "Portfolio Rebalancing Usually Reduces Returns, But Also Risk." Michael Kitces, 23 December 2015, https://www.kitces.com/blog/how-rebalancing-usually-reduces-long-term-returns-but-is-good-risk-management-anyway/.

Kloepfer, Jay. "Periodic Table." Callan, https://www.callan.com/periodic-table/.

"Life expectancy at birth, at 65 years of age, and at 75 years of age, by race and sex." CDC, https://www.cdc.gov/nchs/data/hus/2010/022.pdf.

"Life expectancy at birth, total (years) | Data." World Bank Data, https://data.worldbank.org/indicator/SP.DYN.LE00.IN. Accessed 3 August 2022.

"Medicare Part D: A First Look at Prescription Drug Plans in 2020 - Issue Brief." KFF, 14 November 2019, https://www.kff.org/report-section/medicare-part-d-a-first-look-at-prescription-drug-plans-in-2020-issue-brief/.

"Modern Portfolio Theory (MPT) Definition." Investopedia, https://www.investopedia.com/terms/m/modernportfoliotheory.asp.

Morgan, JP. "Eotm the agony and the ecstasy." J.P. Morgan Private Bank, https://privatebank.jpmorgan.com/content/dam/jpm-wm-aem/global/pb/en/insights/eye-on-the-market/eotm-the-agony-and-the-ecstasy.pdf.

"Mortality in the United States, 2017." CDC, https://www.cdc.gov/nchs/data/databriefs/db328-h.pdf.

"A New Gauge on the Value Financial Advisors Deliver." Investment Planning Counsel, https://www.investmentplanningcounsel.ca/web/guest//archive/article/757576.

"The Other Side of Value: The Gross Profitability Premium - Robert Novy-MarxŽ June, 2012." Robert Novy-Marx, http://rnm.simon.rochester.edu/research/OSoV.pdf.

Parker, Jason R. "The top four questions to ask before taking Social Security." Retirement Budget Calculator, 20 January 2021, https://retirementbudgetcalculator.com/blog.php?post=no-retirement-budget-is-complete-without-factoring.

Pechter, Kerry. "The Pfau Phenomenon." Retirement Income Journal, 10 October 2019, https://retirementincomejournal.com/article/the-pfau-phenomenon/.

Pfau, Wade Donald. Safety-First Retirement Planning: An Integrated Approach for a Worry-Free Retirement. Retirement Researcher Media, 2019.

"Rebalancing Frequency." Retirement Researcher, https://retirementresearcher.com/rebalancing-frequency/..

"Retirement & Survivors Benefits: Life Expectancy Calculator." Social Security, https://www.ssa.gov/oact/population/longevity.html..

"Retirement & Survivors Benefits: Life Expectancy Calculator." Social Security, https://www.ssa.gov/OACT/population/longevity.html. 2.

"A rule for all seasons: Vanguard's dynamic approach to retirement spending." Vanguard Canada, https://www.vanguard.ca/documents/literature/dynamic-ret-spending-paper.pdf.

Sharkansky, Stefan. "Personal Fund." Personal Fund: Home, http://personalfund.com.

"Sound Retirement Planning." Sound Retirement Planning - A Retirement Plan Designed To Help You Achieve Clarity, Confidence & Freedom, https://soundretirementplanning.com/.

Stanley, Thomas J., and William D. Danko. The Millionaire Next Door: The Surprising Secrets of America's Wealthy. Taylor Trade Publishing, 2010.

Stovall, Sam. "A Question of (Re)balance." AAII, https://www.aaii.com/journal/article/10629-a-question-of-rebalance.

"Trinity study." Wikipedia, https://en.wikipedia.org/wiki/Trinity_study.

"231 Taking The Mystery Out of Medicare with Dr. Katy Votava." Sound Retirement Planning, 13 February 2020, http://soundretirementplanning.com/231-taking-the-mystery-out-of-medicare-with-dr-katy-votava.